RECRUITING
GOOD
COLLEGE FACULTY

RECRUITING GOOD COLLEGE FACULTY

Practical Advice for a Successful Search

Baron Perlman

Lee I. McCann

University of Wisconsin-Oshkosh

Anker Publishing Company, Inc.
Bolton, MA

Recruiting Good College Faculty
Practical Advice for a Successful Search

ISBN 1-882982-11-8

Composition by Deerfoot Studios
Cover design by Deerfoot Studios

Anker Publishing Company, Inc.
176 Ballville Road
P.O. Box 249
Bolton, MA 01740-0249

DEDICATION

To Miriam; Les, Larry, and Lowell; and Lester and Cleo—
for lifelong support, tolerance, and encouragement.
L. I. M.

For Joshuah, Nathaniel, and Sandy.
B. P.

ABOUT THE AUTHORS

BARON PERLMAN received his BA from Lawrence University and his PhD in clinical psychology from Michigan State University. He is a Rosebush Professor in the Department of Psychology at the University of Wisconsin-Oshkosh. He has a longstanding interest and involvement in the development of faculty, and serves on the university mentoring committee. He is coauthor of two books: *The Academic Intrapreneur* (with Jim Gueths and Don Weber, 1988, Praeger) and *Organizational Entrepreneurship* (with Jeffrey R. Cornwall, 1990, Irwin). His research focuses on illuminating the teaching preparation and ongoing mentoring and development of faculty who teach, and how teaching is assessed in the recruitment process. He has served on numerous recruitment committees, and continues to do so.

LEE I. McCANN received his PhD in experimental psychology from Iowa State University. He is Associate Vice Chancellor at the University of Wisconsin-Oshkosh with responsibility for instructional and administrative personnel matters. Dr. McCann has served as chair of the Department of Psychology, and on numerous faculty and administrative search committees. His research examines the effects of graduate experiences and mentoring on the career development of new faculty.

TABLE OF CONTENTS

PREFACE AND ACKNOWLEDGEMENTS

Properly conducted, the search process can be a major asset to administrators and a real satisfaction to others on campus. Improperly conducted, the search process can be a memorably negative experience for all involved (Sommerfeld & Nagely, 1974).

To remain vibrant and viable, colleges and universities must hire and retain good teaching faculty. Our institutions, students, curriculum, professional disciplines, and current faculty all benefit from the presence of colleagues who can teach well and who will meet all of the other expectations for contract renewal and tenure. The hiring and retention of good teachers need not be antithetical to hiring faculty who are also good scholars or artistic performers.

THE BOOK

We are pleased that you want to learn about recruiting a good faculty member. Each chapter in the book stands relatively independent so that readers may seek out information as needed in the recruitment process. The book contains three major sections, each of which deals with a different aspect of recruiting good faculty:

1) Part 1, *An Educational Context for Recruiting,* recommends an understanding of recruitment and the faculty role within the context of ethical practice and thoughtful planning.

2) Part 2, *Good Teaching and Scholarship,* reviews the process by which you can begin to determine the unique nature of the position to be filled, emphasizing its teaching responsibilities.

3) Part 3, *The Search,* provides information on the process of hiring a good teaching faculty member. It describes the nuts and bolts of running a smooth and successful search.

We are not attorneys and, since federal and state laws differ and change constantly, we recommend that readers familiarize themselves with the laws, institutional procedures, and policies relevant to their recruitment situation.

Definitions and Focus

- *Department.* The academic unit responsible for recruiting, such as a Department of Physics or English. For those in large departments this term may mean an "interest group." In smaller institutions the recruiting unit may be a multi-disciplinary division.

- *PhD or Doctorate.* The appropriate terminal degree for the position to be filled. For some disciplines a master's degree may be the appropriate educational threshold; for others, postdoctorate experience may be required.

- *Colleges and Universities.* The institution in which you work—a major university, regional university, liberal arts college, junior college, or a vocational/technical institute or high school. We have attempted to provide materials on recruitment which generalize across academic institutions.

- *Renewal.* The extension of a contract.

- *Scholarship.* The research and artistic activity in which many academicians engage.

How To Read This Book

Take from the book that which is relevant and useful for you. No recruiting effort incorporates all of the ideas and materials discussed in this book. To do so would overwhelm recruitment committee members and candidates. Instead, the book presents an ideal recruitment. Use its contents to review and evaluate your current practices and as a source of ideas to maintain or improve them. Oftentimes only one or two ideas, properly implemented, can greatly improve your recruitment process.

The focus in the book is on hiring a tenure-line assistant professor, but the material applies to hiring *ad hoc* faculty, academic staff, senior faculty with tenure, and teaching assistants.

Audience

This book is written for several audiences. First, faculty members responsible for recruiting will find the questions, exercises, and description of recruitment relevant and useful. Second, deans, department chairs, and other administrators can use this book as a source of ideas and suggestions to help their faculty recruit good teaching colleagues. Third, doctoral students and other individuals seeking academic positions can find information about how to obtain an academic position, and what to expect in the process. This book should be invaluable for all of these people.

ACKNOWLEDGEMENTS

Jack Wakeley, acting Chancellor at Western Carolina University, provided assistance as we thought about planning and other topics throughout the book. We also thank Marty Finkler, James Grine, Frank Igov, and Susan McFadden for helping us cover all of the recruiting bases so that the content of the book generalizes across institutions and disciplines. Patricia Keith-Spiegel contributed in the matter of ethics, Mary Koepp taught us about affirmative action, Patricia Koll provided ideas on mentoring, John Tallman educated us on the legalities of recruitment, and John Zubizarreta expanded our knowledge on teaching portfolios. Finally our thanks to the junior college, college, and university faculty members and staff who responded to our request for institutional materials and procedures on hiring.

Baron Perlman
Lee I. McCann

REFERENCE

Sommerfeld, R., & Nagely, D. (1974). Seek and ye shall find: The organization and conduct of a search committee. *Journal of Higher Education, 45,* 239-252.

I

AN EDUCATIONAL CONTEXT
FOR RECRUITING

RECRUITING IN HIGHER EDUCATION

How experienced are you in recruiting? How successful have past depart-mental recruiting efforts been? Was enough attention paid to candidates' teaching abilities? To whom are recruitment committees responsible, and what are they responsible for?

Faculties…directly influence the personal development and ideals of a large fraction of each successive generation, and they prepare these same people for a wide range of vocations, including virtually all the positions of leadership and technical competence in our society (Bowen & Schuster, 1986).

RECRUITING FOR A FACULTY POSITION

If you recruit well and your colleague stays in your department for a period of time, the selection of a new hire is easily a million-dollar decision. Given the importance of this decision, it is important that the recruiting process be well-planned and well-executed. Recruitment is a time-consuming, complex task, and few faculty members recruit often enough to master its intricacies. In addition, it is hard work, requiring many important decisions and offering many opportunities for costly mistakes.

The purpose of this book is to guide you through this process, and to provide a variety of ideas and suggestions related to its various steps. Our discussion emphasizes teaching, which has often received little attention in higher education, especially in the recruitment process. Perhaps it is so visible, prevalent, and important that we have lost sight of it.

Responsibilities to Institution, Discipline, Students, and Self

In recruiting, your responsibilities lie in four domains.

3

1) *Institution.* Since faculty are often defined as the heart and soul of a college or university, you serve your institution by hiring the best person you can. The dilemma, of course, is to define *best*, and we hope to help you answer this question.

2) *Academic discipline.* Good teaching faculty motivate students, recruit majors for a department, and represent a discipline in the classroom. If colleagues are boring teachers, students define the discipline as boring. If colleagues teach without affect or enthusiasm, students think of music, chemistry, psychology, or philosophy as dusty and irrelevant to their lives.

3) *Students.* Many students will spend many hours in the classroom with your new faculty member, and more time reading and writing their assignments. Class by class, course by course, what students receive becomes their education, with each faculty member contributing to what it means to be college educated in our society. From another perspective, students and their parents work hard to afford the costs of a college education; an education society demands now. You want to recruit teaching faculty who can deliver both in the classroom and in their other work with students.

4) *Your colleagues and legacy.* Lastly, "The process by which a department replaces its members and maintains its immortality is as nearly central to an understanding of academic institutions as anything can be" (Caplow & McGee, 1958). The faculty you recruit become your colleagues, members of your academic unit, and potentially your friends. One of the authors was given an academic gown shortly after he arrived at his present institution by a beloved senior colleague. Two decades later, wearing this gown still elicits fond memories of that colleague, and serves as a symbolic tie to the previous academic generation.

Current Recruiting Practices: Not Always This Way

The current method of recruiting, which many young faculty take as *the* way to recruit, is relatively new (see Burke, 1987, and Caplow & McGee, 1958, for descriptions of the history of recruitment). In the 1950s many positions generated 10 or fewer applicants, and while personal contact with writers of recommendations is still important, it was much more so four decades ago (Caplow & McGee, 1958). In the 1950s fewer than half the finalists were interviewed prior to being hired; now the interview is a major step in the selection process. Doctoral school prestige, still important, was critical in the 1950s, and the importance of institutional prestige made hiring closed and preferential. Getting a job in higher education used to depend on what doctoral institution one attended and whom one knew. Open hiring, buttressed by affirmative action and equal opportunity, is a relatively new phenomenon.

Interestingly, as Burke (1987) summarizes the changes in faculty recruitment over 30 years, she notes more advertising, larger applicant pools, greater attention to the candidate's work, more importance of the campus interview, and greater expectation new faculty will influence the department. She never mentions increased attention to teaching abilities and potential.

Professional Responsibilities: The Faculty Role

Faculty are members of an academic community. The multiple professional responsibilities inherent in this membership include good teaching, contributing to an institution's community of scholars or artistic performers in the fine arts, and service.

Recruiting a good teacher. Many college and university faculty members teach well, care about their students' education, and pay attention to good teaching. One relatively new faculty member in a large Southern state university reports that while scholarship expectations are high and will remain so, expectations for good teaching are rising. Faculty are increasingly expected to give more attention to students and to document and think about teaching. To maintain and improve the quality of teaching in higher education, recruitment committees must emphasize good teaching in their selection criteria and decisions to a greater degree than ever before.

In focusing on the ability or potential to teach well, three issues must be kept in mind. First, despite the stereotype of a leisurely professorial career in one's office, studio, or laboratory with minimal student contact, most faculty spend a great deal of time teaching. Teaching takes an average of 64% of faculty time, and as high as 70% in community colleges (Bowen & Schuster, 1986).

Second, recruiting faculty also must remember that the cohort of students has changed over the past decades. Older students are now typical, and part-time students and commuter students are more common. More students reflect a wide spread in ethnic and social background, gender, high school preparation, and commitment to a full-time education than was formerly the case. In hiring new faculty expected to teach well, the demographics of the student body must be factored into the selection equation.

Third, hiring a good teacher can be tricky. It takes years to become a good teacher and mastery of subject matter, while necessary for good teaching, is not sufficient. Faculty must develop the structure and goals of their courses, know how to lecture and lead discussions, and how to reach and educate their students. To these ends teaching is not fixed, but changes depending on variables such as the subject matter, the students, the level of the course, or the setting. Good teaching or the potential to teach well may be more difficult to judge than good scholarship, and even the most conscientious recruitment committee may be more confident in the scholarly or artistic abilities of new hires than in their teaching potential.

Scholarship and artistic performance. Scholarship can involve the discovery of new knowledge, its synthesis, or its application. These efforts may be done alone or collaboratively with students. Scholarship is very important to many faculty and "...the conflict over the value to be assigned to teaching and research has never fully been resolved" (Boyer, 1987, p. 125).

Service, citizenry, governance. A third class of faculty responsibilities includes campus, community and professional organization service, and governance. Faculty are often perceived as the heart of institutional governance and the core of an institution's culture and soul. One important variety of such service is the recruitment of new faculty colleagues.

THE ESSENTIAL LESSONS OF RECRUITING

In order to find and hire those individuals most capable of performing well as faculty, we must do a good job in recruiting. If we could distill the most essential principles of recruiting, what would they be? The resulting list would surely include the following:

- The applicant pool is everything. You want to hire the very best person(s) available, but you are not going to hire them if they do not apply. Do everything possible to reach and encourage candidates to make application. You want to end up with the strongest pool of applicants you can possibly develop.

- Be ethical. Always take the high road when you recruit. There is no substitute for treating people fairly and justly. Treat all candidates not only as though they will be people you see from time to time in the future, but as though they will be your colleagues next year.

- While you are interviewing the candidate, the candidate is interviewing the job. Keep in mind that candidates are assessing their treatment by members of the college community, the position's characteristics, the professionalism of the search, and a host of other variables as the recruitment process unfolds.

- Plan before you recruit. Review your situation and needs and prepare for the probable future. If colleagues have left, do not merely replace them. Hire someone who will best meet your future needs.

- Use your selection criteria. Decide what skills or abilities are needed for your position and do not be distracted by other, irrelevant factors. What is important is how candidates fit your needs. Focus on what best serves your students, your curriculum, and your department.

- Start as soon as possible. Get your recruitment underway as soon as possible and prepare necessary forms, letters, and procedures in advance of your need for them.

- Recruiting should be as open as possible. Departments should have no secrets from candidates and vice versa. Honesty should never be compromised when "selling" a position. If the department puts on airs, it is only setting itself up for unhappiness and failure when the truth emerges later. Give candidates as much information as you can, so that if they accept an offer they are making an informed decision and know what is expected of them.

- If teaching is an important part of the position to be filled, get information about it. Learn all you can about the nature of candidates' teaching. Have them write a statement on their teaching and strongly consider requiring a teaching portfolio from all semi-finalists.

- Hire someone who can meet all criteria for contract renewal or tenure. Achieving tenure will require strong teaching, scholarship or artistic performance, and the ability to be collegial. Even if some candidates truly excel in one of these areas, you must seek those applicants who have balanced interests, abilities, and potential, and are good enough in all areas of performance.

- Keep thorough records. Recruiting is a personnel process, and numerous institutional rules require accountability. Attend closely to your record keeping. While record creation is time consuming if done as the recruitment is underway, it is much more arduous when done after the fact.

- Mentoring is very important. Even the best candidates are not a perfect fit when hired, but they will grow into the job with proper support. Help them develop the skills they need to succeed, or you will be recruiting again.

The scenario

A department wished to recruit faculty in a sub-disciplinary area where two faculty, including the program director, had resigned very late in the prior academic year. Before approving recruitment, the dean asked for an external consultant to evaluate the programmatic empha-sis. Using names forwarded by department members, the dean selected a consultant whose charge was wide-ranging, including the divergent concerns of both the department and dean.

In mid-autumn the consultant received departmental materials, visited the campus, and submitted a written report and recommenda-tions 10 weeks later. It was the end of January before the dean approved the recruitment of a program director and insisted that the person be hired with tenure.

- *What problems do you anticipate with this recruitment?*

- *What concerns do you have about proceeding?*

Some answers

Ethical questions are apparent (Chapter 2). Because of long lead times, job announcements could not be published in appropriate disciplinary jour-nals and newspapers until April, with review of applicants' materials to begin May 1st. Offering a position to faculty from another institution this late could be difficult under AAUP recruitment guidelines.

Planning (Chapter 3) for the recruitment could not be done well. While the department had gathered some data and prepared for the consultant's visit, thorough planning could not be accomplished until the nature of the position was known.

Defining the unique nature of the position to be filled (Chapter 4) was problematic. Until the consultant and dean acted, the department did not know the teaching load, the non-teaching responsibilities, or the possibility of release time for administrative work.

The department had recruited recently, understood the components of good teaching (Chapter 5), and had used portions of the teaching portfolio (Chapter 6). However, because of the late date and compressed time frame, it would be difficult to get semi-finalists to create portfolios prior to select-ing finalists and making invitations for campus visits. Evaluating scholarship (Chapter 7) was familiar to the recruitment committee and presented no problems beyond ensuring that the scholarly activity of candidates matched programmatic needs.

The search process also presented problems. The recruitment committee was organized (Chapter 8) very late. Faculty picked to serve had already accepted other commitments and were extremely busy, so the recruitment was viewed as a burden. While committee roles could be easily assigned and rules agreed on, finding meeting times was difficult because the spring semester was already underway, and schedules were set.

Developing a pool of candidates (Chapter 9) presented special problems. Because of the late date, if a small pool resulted there would not be sufficient time to enlarge it. The position had to be structured quickly with little deliberation. Also, the selection criteria of the dean seemed different from those suggested by department, and there was not time to work these differences through. Posting job announcements involved some hurdles. The job description as modified by the dean's office was not well written. Further, to save both money and time, the dean limited publication to single issues of the periodicals used, not the two issues/months the department recommended.

With a small pool, screening candidates (Chapter 10) would proceed smoothly though the very small pool would probably lack a sufficient number of women and minorities. The important questions were whether any candidate would be worthy of a campus visit (Chapter 11) and to what degree time constraints would interfere with a well-structured visit (Chapter 12). For example, by the time candidates visited campus the semester would be over. It would therefore be difficult for students either to meet with applicants or to attend a guest lecture and provide feedback to the recruitment committee.

The department's recommendation to the dean was to delay the search (Chapter 13) until the following fall semester to obtain a bigger and more diverse pool of applicants more likely to fit department needs. By postponing the search, more attention could be given to the recruitment, and the chances of finding someone to hire who would have a good chance of succeeding in the position (Chapter 14) would be better.

REFERENCES AND RECOMMENDED READINGS

Bloom, A. (1987). *The closing of the American mind.* New York, NY: Touchstone.

Bowen, H. R. (1982). *The state of the nation and the agenda for higher education.* San Francisco, CA: Jossey-Bass.

Bowen, H. R., & Schuster, J. H. (1986). *American professors: A national resource imperiled.* New York, NY: Oxford University Press.

Boyer, E. L. (1987). *The undergraduate experience in America.* New York, NY: Harper & Row.

Boyer, E.L. (1990). *Scholarship reconsidered.* Princeton, NJ: Carnegie Foundation for the Advancement of Teaching.

Burke, D. L. (1987). The academic marketplace in the 1980s: Appointment and termination of assistant professors. *The Review of Higher Education, 10*, 199-214.

Caplow, T., & McGee, R. J. (1958). *The academic marketplace.* New York, NY: Basic Books.

Carnegie Foundation for the Advancement of Teaching. (1981). *Three thousand futures: The next twenty-five years for higher education.* San Francisco, CA: Jossey-Bass.

Chicago Tribune. (1992, June 21-25). *Degrees of neglect: Our failing colleges.*

Clark, B. R. (1987). *The academic life.* Princeton, NJ: Carnegie Foundation for the Advancement of Teaching.

Davidson, C.I., & Ambrose, S. A. (1994). *The new professor's handbook: A guide to teaching and research in engineering and science.* Bolton, MA: Anker.

Deneef, A. L., Goodwin, C. D., & McCrate, E. S. (Eds.). (1988). *The academic's handbook.* Durham, NC: Duke University Press.

Flood, B. J., & Moll, J. K. (1990). *The professor business: A teaching primer for faculty.* Medford, NJ: Learning Information.

Getman, J. (1992). *In the company of scholars: The struggle for the soul of higher education.* Austin, TX: University of Texas Press.

Gibson, G. W. (1992). *Good start: A guidebook for new faculty in liberal arts colleges.* Bolton, MA: Anker.

Smith, P. (1990). *Killing the spirit: Higher education in America.* New York, NY: Viking.

Sykes, C. J. (1986). *Profscam.* New York, NY: St. Martin's Press.

Winston, G. C. (1994, September/October). Teaching: Moral failure or market pressure? *Change,* 9-15.

Zanna, M. P., & Darley, J. M. (Eds.). (1987). *The compleat academic: A practical guide for the beginning social scientist.* Hillsdale, NJ: Lawrence Erlbaum.

2

ETHICAL GUIDELINES
FOR RECRUITING

Think back to when you were hired in your present academic position. How were you treated? Regardless of how long ago that was, is there anything that still elicits bad feelings? Were you treated in some way you thought was questionable from an ethical perspective? Now think back to other positions you applied for, including those you did not get, and ask yourself the same questions. How could those recruitment committees have done things better?

Talk to the most recent faculty recruits in your department and ask how they were treated. Were there any situations which arose which struck them as ethically questionable—instances in which they felt they were mistreated in some way? These newer colleagues can be very helpful to your recruitment committee in offering advice on how to improve the ethical treatment of those you will be recruiting.

INTRODUCTION TO ETHICAL RECRUITING

Ethics involve moral responsibilities, judgments of values, and obligations. They describe how one should behave. The goal of ethical precepts is to systematize and in some ways make impersonal, basic moral imperatives. We need a useable checklist of how to behave which clearly and simply lays out the domain of acceptable, fair behavior and allows us to anticipate, plan for, and deal with potential problems. Before we present a list of ethical principles for recruiting, we will review some reasons why such principles are important.

Not all troublesome behavior is necessarily unethical. The goal of any recruitment committee and department is treatment of candidates which is not only ethical, but also decent, fair, and honorable. At the least everyone should:

- Meet legal requirements when recruiting. An example would be observing state or federal equal opportunity or affirmative action laws which require equal consideration of all candidates, regardless of race, sex, or disability. We do not propose that those recruiting become legal experts, but they should be familiar with laws which apply to their recruitment work.

- Act responsibly. Lacking the competence, skills, or abilities to recruit probably is not unethical, but it can negatively affect other people. For example, being sloppy about reimbursement or losing submitted materials is poor recruitment practice, but not unethical.

- Act professionally. Normal etiquette should be practiced. We all are familiar with examples of the indignities faculty applicants have suffered because of irresponsible and unprofessional behavior on the part of those recruiting (e.g., Trela, 1989). For example, it is discourteous for a dean to be over an hour late for an interview with a candidate.

The responsibility for an ethical, professional, and responsible recruitment lies with the entire department. The recruitment committee should seriously consider educating its departmental colleagues about ethical matters since many persons in addition to members of the committee will interact with the candidates. Part of this education must be the establishment of a departmental culture where no unethical behavior will be tolerated.

Why Ethics?

Ethical conduct in recruiting is important for several reasons.

- There is a long history in higher education of the professoriate serving as role models for others, both students and citizens outside academe. In the present instance, we are also modeling appropriate behaviors for applicants and colleagues, and probably students as well.

- Integrity is important in all interpersonal interactions; it is the foundation on which trust and confidence are based. For example, faculty cannot decry the scandals in college athletics across the nation and then themselves act unethically when, out of the limelight, they use questionable procedures in the recruitment of a new colleague.

- Recruitment affects people's lives. Those who serve on recruitment committees exercise a great deal of power over the lives and futures of applicants. This power must not be misused.

- The probability of a trouble free search resulting in the hiring and retention of a good teacher is enhanced by conducting recruitment activities within an ethical context.

- We hypothesize that a newly recruited colleague who has been treated well will be happier, more productive, and more likely to stay.

Ethical Leadership

To recruit well, one must be continuously sensitive to ethical considerations. Ethical conduct is every faculty member's responsibility during a recruitment, but we recommend that a member of the recruitment committee be formally chosen for the role of ethical officer, with the responsibility of raising issues of ethical behavior and procedure as the recruitment process unfolds. Working through ethical issues as they arise, and before the committee acts, is much easier than having to confront them after a mistake has been made. An ethical leader assists colleagues in defining an ethical issue and considering alternative ways of behaving. We recommend that the recruitment committee openly consider any ethical issues that arise and then act on its collective judgment and conscience. When we recruit, we can usually identify *right* and *wrong* behaviors without difficulty, but at times there may be no one right answer and ethical precepts may be in conflict, one with another. At such times, a formal discussion and committee decision will increase the chance that proper choices will be made.

Ethics as Practical Action Guides

We do not propose to answer all of the important ethical questions related to recruiting, but we will present six basic principles—ethical do's and don'ts—and call your attention to some common sense, moral principles applicable to the recruitment process. These ethical principles are best thought of as starting points for the development of procedures and policies to guide your recruitment activities, and to assist in the solution of ethical problems when they arise.

Faculty members who serve on recruitment committees want to maximize the applicants' positive experiences and minimize any problems for both applicants and recruiting faculty. Following a standard of personal integrity in interactions within and beyond the university is a large step toward ensuring an ethical recruitment process.

The ethical principles we propose carry no weight nor sanctions beyond being the right thing to do. They reflect what should be a common understanding and practice of desirable behavior. Our goal is to identify a few clear, consistent, basic principles, acceptable to the reader. If we err, it is on the side of simplicity. Examples are provided for illumination and discussion. They include an empathic component regarding how those recruited like to be treated, and how we would want to be treated were we looking for an academic position. Of course, readers must also follow any additional professional or discipline-specific ethical standards applicable to them.

ETHICAL PRINCIPLES FOR RECRUITING

The AAUP*Redbook* (AAUP, 1990) contains a general *Statement on Professional Ethics* recognizing that "…membership in the academic profession carries with it special responsibilities" (p.75) including respect for associates and their opinions. In all of the writings on ethics, and especially ethics in the academic setting, the most relevant for our purposes is a statement on *The Ethics of Recruitment and Faculty Appointment* adopted by the Council of Colleges of Arts and Sciences (CCAS) in November, 1992 and jointly adopted by the American Association of University Professors (AAUP) in June, 1993. Unfortunately, many academics are unfamiliar with these ethical guidelines. Guidelines or examples below which are cited from this statement are referenced as (CCAS).

PRINCIPLE 1
EQUAL TREATMENT

All candidates must be treated equally. Ethical recruitment implies fair treatment. For example, when recruiting, we must avoid halo effects for candidates personally recommended by someone we know or someone with whom we are familiar. We may look closely at such credentials, but no more closely than we review those of other applicants. Personal attachments to candidates or their mentors could potentially distort the fairness of the recruitment process. Candidates should not be rated highly simply because someone well-known has written a letter of recommendation. In brief, treat candidates identically. Other examples of equality in the recruitment of candidates include:

- Expect all candidates to follow position announcement instructions in submitting materials. If you require a statement on teaching, candidates who fail to submit this statement should be asked to do so.

- Provide all candidates with identical information about the position and the search process. There is no place for inside information.

- Avoid illegal questions, such as marital status or age.

- If a finalist wishes to talk with the person who previously held the position, all finalists should be able to do so.

- Make no decisions before the announced closing date for applications.

- Treat all candidates the same during an interview. There should be no tough campus visit for one candidate, nor creampuff treatment for another.

- Abstain from recruitment decisions on candidates in whom you have a personal interest.

- Avoid discrimination. Discrimination is illegal, and all those recruiting, especially the ethical leader, should be sensitive to it.

- Apply salary ranges included in the position description equally to all candidates.

- Make mentoring equally available to anyone who is hired.

PRINCIPLE 2
MAINTAIN CLARITY AND STABILITY OF CRITERIA AND PROCEDURES

The process and criteria used in recruitment should be clearly stated, consistent, and objective. Vague and secret procedures generate confusion and, at times, antagonism. To meet this ethical goal, the recruitment committee must operationally define selection criteria. The process of defining desirable candidate traits and experiences improves the reliability and validity of selection and minimizes criticism. What is needed is agreement by all administrators and faculty involved regarding the major criteria for the position (CCAS), from the beginning of the process. For example, instead of stating in a position announcement that maturity is highly valued, one could emphasize that candidates should have teaching experience, a broad background in their discipline (a major in the discipline at the bachelor's level required or highly desirable), and intellectual interests beyond the major area of study. Keep useable notes on the process and procedures of a search to provide tangible evidence of clear and stable recruitment practices. Other examples of clarity and stability of criteria include:

- Agree on what a new faculty member is expected to do before hiring.

- If applicants should possess special qualities, identify these criteria in position descriptions and job announcements and survey all applicants for these qualities.

- Stick to selection criteria. If candidates are expected to be interested in developing into even better teachers (e.g., use of Teaching Center, reading, videotaping classes), this criterion should not be abandoned for faculty who feel little need to work at the art and craft of teaching.

- Evaluate all candidate credentials with rating forms and criteria all recruitment committee members can reliably use.

- Evaluate numerical ratings of student evaluations/opinions of teaching within a context. Ask for normative data.

- Establish the same or similar conditions for each campus visitor performing regular, one-on-one, or master class teaching.

- Develop a rating form so that teaching (videotapes, during campus visit) is evaluated using consistent criteria.

- Do not ask for information in letters of reference which is irrelevant to the criteria used in selection of finalists.

- Ask all candidates the same basic questions.

PRINCIPLE 3
MAINTAIN CONFIDENTIALITY

Confidentiality must be maintained (CCAS). Candidates need to know to what extent information about their application, and even the fact they have applied for a position, will remain confidential. Tell candidates if your state has sunshine laws under which all applicants for a state position must be disclosed. Once a statement of confidence is made, it *must* be implemented. Discretion within the searching department is necessary, and members must keep discussions of candidates among themselves. Nothing can create discord as quickly as gossip, or statements taken out of context. The academic community is tightly knit, and no one is well-served if perceptions of candidates' credentials are communicated to candidates (or others) informally, whether what was said was positive or negative.

The principle of confidentiality applies particularly to recruitment committee members. They must be able to communicate candidly knowing that what is said will stay within the meeting. Only then is free communication possible. Other examples of confidentiality include:

- Keep all application materials and correspondence secure and available only to those with a need to know. This confidentiality extends to teaching statements and other portfolio materials.

- Respect the wishes of employed candidates who do not want employers or colleagues to know they are seeking a new position. Communications should be sent to an applicant's home address. Similarly, applicants should be asked where they would like to be telephoned or receive e-mail, and their wishes should be respected.

PRINCIPLE 4
MAINTAIN HONESTY AND INTEGRITY IN COMMUNICATION

All members of the recruiting department and institution must strive for honest communication with applicants. Ethical recruitment avoids deceptive or misleading statements. Honest and open communication may be more difficult than you imagine depending on the needs of the individuals at the various levels of your institution involved in a search. You must be sure that members of the recruitment committee have the facts straight. Statements regarding teaching load and other responsibilities must be consistent with the position description and other written position information. All search committee members must communicate the same information to candidates, as should the department chairperson, dean, and provost. Those we recruit expect us to be truthful; important decisions are made based on what we tell them. Other examples of "candor and effective communication" (CCAS) include:

- Do not advertise for positions already filled. Searches must be genuine, and sham searches are unethical.

- If teaching is an important criterion in hiring, communicate this to applicants.

- Avoid misleading materials. Do not send a brochure with a picture of the new music studio and imply it is representative of physical space if 80% of studio space is older and less well-equipped.

- Do not wait for candidates to ask questions. Applicants from the private sector and some new PhDs may not know what to ask. Freely share the entire range of professorial responsibilities expected of someone you will hire including in classroom work, out-of-classroom teaching, advising, grant writing, scholarly efforts, studio work, ensemble or collaborative music performance, department and institutional service, and community service.

- Provide accurate information on housing costs, health insurance programs, etc.

- Accurately represent the abilities, motivation, and nature of students.

- Accurately describe the strengths and weaknesses of the curriculum and possibilities for teaching new courses. Expect debate between committee members on these issues.

- State teaching load expectations and the nature of teaching (e.g., large lectures, small seminars, tutorials) honestly. If a lesser teaching load is available only with buy downs for administrative work, scholarship, or service, make this known to applicants.

- Honestly describe fiscal support for teaching, artistic endeavors, or scholarship. If start-up funds are probably the only such monies candidates will ever have, tell them so.

- Be honest about threats to your department, and to good teaching or scholarship. At the same time, while not overselling, be honest about opportunities as well.

- Inform candidates (finalists), when applicable, if the recruiting department is badly fractured or morale is low. Candidates have a right to know these things so they can make up their own minds. If you can minimize the number of surprises for new hires, you can also maximize the probability that they will stay and you will not have to search again.

- Send letters of appointment in a timely fashion. CCAS guidelines state that candidates shall receive a confirming letter within 10 days of a verbal job offer.

According to CCAS guidelines, an ethical letter of appointment must contain:

- The initial rank

- Whether the appointment is tenure track

- Credit toward tenure and length of the probationary period

- Conditions of renewal

- Salary and benefits

- Duties of the position

- The institution's commitment to start-up

- Date the appointment begins and date when candidate will start work

- Date by which the candidate is expected to respond to the offer (not less than two weeks from its receipt)

- Details of departmental and institutional policy which affect the appointment

PRINCIPLE 5
KEEP PROMISES TO CANDIDATES AND INSTITUTION

Keep promises to your institution and candidates. When we recruit, we are making a promise to our department and institution to hire someone who will meet current or anticipated student, curricular, and institutional needs. To keep this promise, recruiting faculty strive to match the department's goals and needs with the applicant's abilities. A good fit between the two is essential to a successful recruitment. At the same time, the institution must keep its promises. For example, positions should remain funded once announced, and support for a newly hired faculty member should be provided as promised. Other examples of promise-keeping include:

- Inform candidates that verbal assurances, while given in good faith, will be put in writing if and when the candidate is offered a position.

- Tell finalists that conditions of employment may be subject to change in the years ahead.

- Keep all promises for campus visit reimbursement.

- Make appointments in binding letters, not orally (CCAS).

- Do everything you can to ensure that your expectations for teaching and scholarship can be met. In order to teach well, new colleagues need support. For example, avoid giving them numerous service responsibilities during their first year or two.

- Mentor new faculty.

PRINCIPLE 6
DO NO HARM

Respect the welfare of others. Recruitment must display a positive regard for the well-being of others. We should not harm candidates, our students, or a curriculum. Similarly, candidates should do no harm. CCAS guidelines state that no appointments should be made later than May 1 and that no faculty should resign in order to accept other employment later than May 15. While special cases are recognized, these specific dates serve two purposes. First, they make it unethical for academic recruitment committees to poach faculty from other programs at a late date. Second, they protect academic programs and students from faculty members with scheduled courses and other responsibilities (e.g., collaborative scholarship, independent studies), who wish to leave when it is too late to replace them. Other examples of doing no harm include:

- Make sure members of a search committee agree to work even if outside the normal semester/academic year. Stopping or delaying a search because faculty refuse to work during an extended break delays hiring, prolongs the ambiguity for applicants, and may allow strong candidates to be hired by someone else.

- Avoid labeling people as protected or minority in a way which reduces dignity or self worth. Applicant attributes, talents, and relative weaknesses are simply these and nothing more.

- Do not exploit candidates during interviews. Ask hard questions in a spirit of respect. Badgering candidates is neither professional nor ethical. One should not enhance one's reputation as a curmudgeon at the expense of candidates; such behavior is exploitive.

- Stringing candidates along is unprofessional and unethical. Tell unsuccessful candidates as soon as possible that they have not been moved to your list of finalists, or have not been selected from this list for a campus visit. This ends their uncertainty and allows them to pursue other options.

- The letter to candidates who have been removed from consideration, even if a form letter, should be supportive, thanking them for expressing interest in your department and position.

EQUAL OPPORTUNITY AND THE AFFIRMATIVE ACTION TIGHTROPE

Equal opportunity employment practices carry legal weight and do not conflict with the ethical principles we have proposed. However, affirmative action, that is, attempting to make up for and overcome discrimination in the hiring of protected groups and increase their numbers in the professorate, may present ethical and moral dilemmas for recruitment committees. These problems arise because the philosophical underpinnings for affirmative action contain a number of complicated assumptions and an ethical analysis of affirmative action involves multiple, and often differing, perspectives on the meanings of justice (e.g., fairness, freedom, the greatest good)

(Taylor, 1991). We do not have definitive answers but recommend that you (1) carefully consider the needs of your students, curriculum, and department, and (2) strive to conduct a search process which appropriately reflects these needs. A more complete discussion of the cultural and legal aspects of affirmative action and its ethical analyses may be found in Taylor (1991). Examples of ethical practices related to equal opportunity and affirmative action include:

- Seriously consider only candidates who have potential to be selected.

- Do not keep candidates in the pool solely for "diversity." However, when making decisions on candidates, continue consideration of those who attended or worked at relatively unknown institutions or who have more unusual career paths if they are among the last to be cut. Keeping such candidates in the pool allows additional opportunity to become familiar with their credentials and serves all candidates well, but especially those from protected groups.

- Make every effort to ensure that assigned teaching responsibilities do not inadvertently exclude a protected candidate. If laboratory instruction is required and the facilities are not easily accessible, reasonable efforts should be made to arrange access for a disabled candidate.

- Hiring someone with an international status and an inability to teach in understandable English to fill a position and/or meet affirmative action guidelines is not uncommon, but its ethical status is questionable.

- Do not assume someone from a protected group has an inherent interest in teaching courses involving content on cultural or ethnic diversity. Assigning such teaching responsibilities without talking with the new hire first is unethical.

CANDIDATE ETHICS

Candidates also bear ethical responsibilities during the recruitment process, since the behavior of candidates can affect the welfare of a searching department. Examples of ethical behavior for candidates include:

- Candidates should inform search committees about conditions which bear upon their acceptance of a job (CCAS) such as equipment requests or needs, or a delayed start-up date.

- Candidates should not work their way through recruitment, interview, and perhaps an offer with the primary motivation of obtaining a free trip to that part of the country, and/or to return to the home institution and use the offer to leverage greater salary or other benefits. Such manipulation is reprehensible but not uncommon. We know of one faculty member who applied to a number of institutions in which he had little interest, and with several campus visits arranged a free trip across the western United States.

- Candidates' submitted works (papers, artistic productions, etc.) must be their own.

- Authorship order of scholarly work should accurately reflect the contribution to the research and writing.

- Statements on past teaching should accurately reflect course responsibilities.

- Teaching statements in the teaching portfolio must be written by the candidate.

CHECKLIST

_____ The Council of Colleges of Arts and Sciences and AAUP ethical guidelines have been read.

_____ How your last few junior colleagues were recruited has been investigated, and any ethical problems identified.

_____ A member of the recruitment committee has been identified to be responsible for ethics as the ethical leader.

_____ The following ethical guidelines are understood.

    _____ Equality

    _____ Clarity and stability of criteria and procedures

    _____ Confidentiality

    _____ Honesty and integrity in communication

    _____ Promise keeping to candidate and institution

    _____ Welfare of and respect for others

_____ Equal opportunity and affirmative action will be carefully considered.

EXERCISE

The scenario

You have an ad hoc faculty member working in your department. His teaching is excellent; the individual shows maturity, respect for students, and handles all the stressors of a temporary appointment with aplomb. Your department has been given permission to fill the position with a tenure line, assistant professor. You would like to hire your ad hoc colleague; this person possesses all of the intellectual, personal, and academic traits you would look for in an assistant professor, is an excellent fit for the position, and would apply for and accept the position if it was offered. In other words, you have an "inside" candidate, which is not uncommon in recruitment.

- *What ethical dilemmas does this scenario entail?*

- *The ad hoc colleague is a Caucasian male. What additional ethical dilemmas does this fact cause?*

- *How do you ethically recruit in this situation? What broad guidelines would you use?*

Some answers

The Principles of Maintaining Equality, and Maintaining Clarity and Stability of Criteria advise that this person's credentials be given the same consideration as anyone else. At the least, you will learn if he really is the most qualified for the position. On the other hand, you could learn that, initial impressions notwithstanding, there are other candidates with equal or greater potential to do the job. The Principle of Maintaining Confidentiality argues that no special communication be given to this candidate, and that search committee members divulge no more information to this candidate than to any other. The Principle of Maintaining Honesty and Integrity in Communication and Behavior suggests you tell other applicants, if they ask, that there is someone in the department applying for the position.

Promise Keeping as an ethical Principle argues that the search committee keep program and curricular needs clearly in mind. The in-house candidate remains viable only if his credentials and abilities provide excellent potential for serving students and the department well. And, of course, no promises should be made to this candidate which cannot be kept. Finally, the expectations of affirmative action support the conclusion that the recruitment committee must give a protected group candidate's credentials a close reading. It may find an equally qualified candidate who has the additional advantage of offering students personal experiences and perspectives on what is taught which complements or improves the department, especially if the department is mostly comprised of Caucasian men.

REFERENCES AND RECOMMENDED READINGS

American Association of University Professors. (1990). *Policy documents and reports*. Washington, DC: Author.

Council of Colleges of Arts and Sciences. (1992). *The ethics of recruitment and faculty appointment*. Columbus, OH: The Ohio State University.

Dill, D. D. (Ed.). Ethics and the academic profession. *Journal of Higher Education, 53*, 243-381.

Marchese, T. J., & Lawrence, J. F. (Eds.). (1988). *The search committee handbook: A guide to recruiting administrators*. Washington, DC: American Association for Higher Education.

May, W. W. (Ed.). (1990). *Ethics and higher education*. New York, NY: Macmillan.

Steininger, M., Newell, J. D., & Garcia, L. T. (1984). *Ethical issues in psychology*. Homewood, IL: Dorsey Press.

Taylor, B. R. (1991). *Affirmative action at work: Law, politics, and ethics*. Pittsburgh, PA: University of Pittsburgh Press.

Trela, D. J. (1989, March 29). Academic indignities. *Chronicle of Higher Education*, pp. B3-B4.

3

PLANNING: TAKING STOCK AND LOOKING AHEAD

What are the strengths of your department that would make a job there attractive, and what are the problems and weaknesses that would make it difficult to hire and retain a good candidate? What opportunities exist that you might take advantage of to strengthen your department, and what threats must be anticipated and dealt with? Take a moment to make a brief list of these strengths, weaknesses, opportunities, and threats. After reviewing it, do you think that you can conduct a search, bring in a new faculty member, and realistically expect your new hire to succeed?

Can a good teaching faculty member be brought into your department and realistically expect to develop and thrive? What combination of specialized training, skills, abilities, and personal characteristics will best fit your current and future needs? Before turning outward to the screening and selection of candidates, we recommend that you turn inward and take a careful look at your own department.

To answer the questions above, you need to review your departmental history to gain some perspective, evaluate your current situation, and consider your future direction. Recruitment can be an unexpected and often unappreciated opportunity to take stock, evaluate your needs, and plan any necessary changes to your programs and physical facilities.

INTRODUCTION TO PLANNING

In this chapter we present some ideas to help you conduct a systematic review of your current situation so you can better answer these questions, both for your own purposes, and so that you will have an organized and thoughtful response when they are asked by job candidates and/or your dean. In order to maintain your strengths and ameliorate your weaknesses, you first need to identify them. This departmental diagnosis is based upon planning—an organized evaluation and decision-making process. The processes and principles we suggest also are useful in dealing with department problems other than recruiting.

A review of your college and/or division and an attempt to understand where the institution as a whole is heading should also be considered. Perhaps the dean can provide this information, or you might consider meeting with your chief academic officer. Knowing what is receiving special attention and/or funding may affect recruitment decisions. For example, if more interdisciplinary courses are being encouraged, will this affect the way the department describes a position opening?

Departmental Planning

The type of planning we describe is not planning the nuts and bolts of the recruitment process, a subject discussed in Chapters 8 through 14. We are suggesting a general evaluation of your current situation as part of recruiting, and a plan for moving forward from wherever you find yourself. Our special emphasis is on hiring good teachers, and the approach we are suggesting will help you to:

- Evaluate your situation and get your house in order

- Identify your strengths and weaknesses

- Identify and make decisions about your goals and values, and about your curricular offerings

- Decide how much you really value and support good teaching

- Define the type of position to be filled

- Identify the type of person, professional specialization, and pedagogical skills or potential that will best fit the current and future department

Planning rarely takes place, often because we do not feel we have the time to do it. This is shortsighted. We argue for a thoughtful pause to allow you to think and plan, prior to active recruiting.

If you have a retirement or resignation, you may feel that what you need is a nearly identical colleague to fill an obvious curricular hole. Your situation has undoubtedly changed since that person was hired, however, and you should take some time to reevaluate your needs. Even if the position is well-defined, there are many questions related to the department and its future that should be reviewed prior to soliciting and evaluating candidates.

Planning does not ensure that all problems will be solved, but your department will be better off than it might have been without planning, and you will know where you want to go and what to do first to get there.

A Program Review Versus Departmental Planning

Departmental planning is often confused with, or replaced by, a typical departmental program review. However, program reviews and focused planning are very different processes designed to achieve distinct ends. Typically, *Departmental Program Reviews* are:

- Required by the institution

- Completed regularly

- Designed to answer general questions of interest to the administration rather than the more specific questions of most interest to your department

- Quantitative, statistical, and highly rational, using a great deal of data

- Weak in the critical area of implementation and often dependent on unavailable resources to address identified problems

    In contrast, *Departmental Planning* (at its best):

- Is voluntary and carried out as needed

- Can focus on limited or specific questions of immediate concern

- Allows a feeling of control and shared purpose

- Concentrates on the most relevant data

- Encourages honest discussion

- Is inclusive of personalities and politics

- Is more easily translated into outcomes; sometimes only incremental gains are possible, but this is still progress

- Is almost always more focused and useful than institutionally required planning

- Assists in achieving a broad understanding of the past and present, and a consensus on future goals

Questions Planning Will Help Answer

A candidate for a faculty position may ask a variety of questions, and strategic planning assists the department in learning the answers. Even if the candidate does not ask, you want to know the answers anyway! How else are you going to improve your department and your environment for teaching and scholarship/artistic performance? These questions are presented as examples of what departments work on when they plan, and they are divided into two parts. The first set of questions are general issues for a department. The second set more specifically focus on teaching and hiring a good teaching faculty member. The second set are used in planning to get the department thinking about teaching, its curriculum, and the recruitment of a colleague with good teaching skills or abilities. Depending on the department's needs, questions related to scholarship or artistic performance would also be grist for the planning mill.

General questions you might ask could include:

- What are the department's general strengths and weaknesses?

- What should the department guard against changing, and what is it doing well?

- What things need to be changed in the department? What two or three issues must be addressed immediately?

- How should the department allocate faculty, resources, and commitment to its various programs?

- What is the future likely to be, or at least the two or three most likely and desirable alternatives?

Questions you might ask specific to recruitment and teaching include:

- What are the practical consequences of a commitment to higher (or lower) quality curricular offerings?

- What would happen if this faculty position went unfilled?

- Are faculty teaching workloads increasing?

- Are there any patterns apparent after comparing faculty who have been recruited and stayed, with those who left?

- Does the department really value undergraduate teaching?

- How does the department assess its teaching?

- How does the department reward good teaching?

- How do your core courses relate to each other and to the overall curriculum?

- What is the most important course(s) in your curriculum and why?

- What are the most important curricular changes, if any, made in the past 10 years?

- How strong is the curriculum now and what changes are needed?

- How does the curriculum compare to other, more highly ranked departments?

- Does your department overemphasize certain specialty areas, and neglect others of equal or greater importance?

- What have the department's enrollment patterns been in the last five years?

- How well does the department resolve conflicts with students?

GATHERING INFORMATION

There are several ways to gather the information needed for planning and answering questions such as the ones above. We will discuss three: (1) reviewing your literature, (2) using an external consultant, and (3) using structured planning techniques.

Review Your Literature

It is amazing how much you can learn, and how easily, if you merely read what has already been written about your department, its curriculum, and its programs. We suggest reading the following:

- University catalog

- Department handouts to students describing programs and faculty

- Department budgets for the past two or three years

- Brief vitae for each of your faculty, including specialty areas of teaching and scholarly interests. Note the ages of your colleagues as well, since this will be important in anticipating retirements and subsequent personnel needs.

- Recent program reviews

- Other materials relevant to your department, its curriculum, and past history

Use of a Consultant

Program reviews often use an external consultant, who may gather very different data than you want for more specific strategic planning, may interact with the department in a different manner, and/or may have different goals. A consultant for strategic planning can be someone from off campus or a respected and knowledgeable local expert. Such a person may be used for:

- Assistance with a more extensive planning process

- Discussing planning in general and the type best suited to your needs

- Help with a wide variety of departmental issues, such as defining your department and its programs

- Providing an objective evaluation

- Identifying current or anticipated problems

- Focusing on specific concerns such as curricular structure or supporting and encouraging good teaching

- Identifying the decisions that need to be made in order to move forward

- Sampling of opinion

- Leading discussions

- Providing input from a neutral individual

- Controlling vocal, difficult, and/or powerful colleagues so everyone contributes to the decision-making process

If you choose to use a consultant, you need someone familiar with both academia and teaching, and departmental planning. This consultant will help the department consider and understand its:

- History

- Current situation, issues, and problems

- Areas of agreement and disagreement

- Need for curricular revisions

- Options based on what similar departments are doing

- Department administrative (re)organization

- Sequence of future hires reflecting probable retirements and current and future needs

Structured Techniques for Planning: The SWOT (Strengths, Weaknesses, Opportunities, and Threats) Analysis

There are a number of structured techniques for planning that can be used with or without a consultant, and any one of them may suit your purposes. We will describe the use of a SWOT analysis, an approach which has worked well for us. SWOT stands for Strengths, Weaknesses, Opportunities, and Threats. SWOT and other planning processes can be extensive, taking up to a year or more. We present the SWOT analysis as a planning tool for use in a briefer and more focused arena, as a forum for brainstorming and discussion, and as a means to help your department address any of the questions posed above.

A strength is a resource which helps a department realize its goals and succeed in its strategies, and a weakness is anything that hinders the department. A threat is any factor that may limit or impede your department in pursuit of its goals and, conversely, an opportunity offers promise or potential for moving it closer to its identified objectives (Stoner & Fry, 1987).

A SWOT analysis considers both the department's internal and external environment and identifies what needs to be done. It can be used to analyze any specific issue or component of the department. For example, what subspecialty of your discipline should you hire now, and what will be the next position you fill?

The benefit of doing a SWOT analysis is that all ideas and people offering ideas have equal validity, standing, and power, and an equal opportunity to look foolish. The goal is to elicit as many different ideas as possible in order to have the broadest selection from which to work. The questions at the beginning of this chapter asked you to take the simple first step of a SWOT analysis, listing your departmental strengths, weaknesses, opportunities, and threats. Review these notes and identify the three biggest problems your department faces. If you now identify the one you would attempt to fix first, you have just defined a problem that can be addressed.

Doing a SWOT analysis is as simple as that, at least to start. Identify a time when all of your colleagues can get together, and a congenial location. Then engage in a series of brainstorming sessions to list the strengths of your department, your weaknesses, any opportunities you can identify, and any threats you see on the horizon. As you create your lists in each of these categories, be open to even the most trivial suggestions, and list everything. Doing a SWOT analysis in a group allows your colleagues to feed on each other's ideas and produces a great variety of entries. After you have completed this exercise, which can be quite enjoyable, you must take these lists and do something with them.

Moving From SWOT To Action

Group your Ss, Ws, Os, and Ts into categories under specific headings. In our department, prior to recruiting, we assessed our curriculum through use of a SWOT analysis. After analyzing the resulting lists and categorizing them by ideas/subjects, we ended up with area headings for (a) Curriculum (e.g., courses, prerequisites), (b) Resources (e.g., students, faculty, facilities), (c) Out of Classroom Learning (e.g., honorary society, collaborative scholarship, advising), and (d) Data (e.g., do we have accurate information on the number of our majors, minors, service students, the job success of graduates?). This SWOT analysis identified the need to strengthen out of classroom undergraduate learning, and we recruited a new hire with strengths and interests in this area.

After you have reorganized your Ss, Ws, Os, and Ts under subject headings, you must decide what action to take first. In choosing where to begin to improve your department, you might choose:

* The most pressing and important issue

* A task which will take little time whether you succeed or not

* An area where you know you are likely to succeed

We recommend the third option for your first attempt, since success will create good will and a feeling that you have succeeded in improving some aspect of your situation. Pick your topic and have a small group of colleagues propose solutions and do the work. In our case, we chose to develop an advising notebook for both new and existing faculty. This was a simple but positive beginning to the more ambitious projects we tackled later. When you have the energy, move on to the next topic.

For the purposes of this book, you would want to work on the position you will seek to recruit. What type of subspecialty, or combination of specialties is needed, and how will the position fit into your curriculum, long-range needs, and developmental plan?

CHECKLIST

_____ Department has agreed to plan.

_____ Reading about department and curriculum is completed.

_____ Decision reached on use of consultant for more extensive planning.

_____ Department has identified important questions to explore.

_____ SWOT (or alternative planning technique) has elaborated on these questions and identified others for consideration.

_____ Problems for recruitment and retention are identified, and corrective actions initiated.

EXERCISE

The scenario

A department decided to spend some time planning for its future, and an external consultant was located to provide someone neutral with whom to work. The consultant asked each department member to complete a questionnaire to be collected and mailed to her, and on the opening evening of two days of planning, she summarized the results.

The department faculty were pleased to hear that they agreed on the strengths of the curriculum. A supportive and expert secretarial staff was noted, and the department's reputation within the university seemed a good one.

The consultant had asked each faculty member to rank on a one to five scale whether he or she would accept a departmental position which emphasized good teaching. Thirty percent of the faculty said "absolutely not" (You would have to be crazy to expect to do good teaching here. There is no support and the environment is not conducive to good teaching.) or "Probably Not" (I would look closely at other job openings. In the long run it would be too difficult to teach well here.). Another 40% of the department were "Neutral" in responding to this question (This can be a good place to teach and do scholarship but the expectations are high. Some young faculty leave or are greatly stressed because of these expectations.). Only 30% of the faculty answered "Probably Yes" (If I stayed focused and had good mentoring, I could teach well and still meet other responsibilities) or "Yes" (This is a good place to work and one can be a good teacher here.).

- *Where would you start in addressing these data?*
- *What changes are needed, if any, prior to recruiting?*

Some answers

The planning process provided blocks of time for discussion of important issues which arose as a result of working with the consultant. In this case, the issue of the departmental teaching environment needed discussion.

A SWOT analysis was conducted on the place of good teaching within the department. This allowed the department to brainstorm a number of ideas on both the strengths of the department from a teaching perspective, its weaknesses, and opportunities and threats. Department faculty were interested to learn that from a variety of perspectives its teaching really was quite strong. Yet a fairly long list of weaknesses and threats to good teaching was compiled. Some were under the control of the department, others resulted from lack of support by the university. This was the first time the department had ever systematically looked at teaching, and just engaging in the process helped focus on problem areas and energized the faculty.

The last session of the two days of planning focused on the future and how the department wanted to proceed. The teaching environment was selected for improvement, and an ad hoc committee was formed to begin work on what could be done to improve it. While all the weaknesses would not be addressed before the next recruitment was completed, and while some threats could only be acknowledged but not controlled, the department was able to address several problems which were under its control. As a result, the next position to be filled was made more attractive to promising candidates, the teaching situation for all faculty was improved, and the department was better prepared to discuss its teaching environment with candidates.

REFERENCES AND RECOMMENDED READINGS

Kuhn, R. L. (Ed.). (1988). *Handbook for creative and innovative managers.* New York, NY: McGraw-Hill.

Marchese, T. J., & Lawrence, J. F. (1988). *The search committee handbook: A guide to recruiting administrators.* Washington, DC: American Association for Higher Education.

Ray, M., & Myers, R. (1986). *Creativity in business.* Garden City, NY: Doubleday.

Stoner, C. R., & Fry, F. L. (1987). *Strategic planning in the small business.* Cincinnati, OH: South-Western.

Waggaman, J. S. (1983). *Faculty recruitment, retention and fair employment: Obligations and opportunities.* ASHE-ERIC Higher Education Research Report No. 2, Washington, DC: Association for the Study of Higher Education.

II

GOOD TEACHING
AND SCHOLARSHIP

THE UNIQUE NATURE OF
YOUR POSITION

What are the workload expectations for the position you are filling? Are your faculty colleagues performing at the level you will expect of the new hire? Can new faculty in your department meet your definition of good teaching or scholarship given all that they must do, or do you need to modify your workload and performance expectations?

New faculty members are confronted with many tasks and expectations, typically including teaching, scholarship, creative artistic work, and varieties of committee work and other service. Within and beyond these basic responsibilities, each position has unique characteristics better suited to the skills and abilities of only some of the candidates who will apply for your position.

The purpose of this chapter is to review and discuss four factors which must be considered in order to achieve the best possible agreement between the requirements of the position and the characteristics of the person selected to fill it. These factors are (1) the effective teaching load, (2) nonteaching faculty responsibilities, (3) perceptual issues, and (4) departmental and institutional culture.

The outcome of a close look at these factors should be an increased confidence that the position is clearly defined and realistic, and that someone who is a good fit for the position can be hired and retained. The recruitment committee must integrate the material gathered in planning as described in Chapter 3, into its development of the unique position to be filled, and translate this gestalt into a realistic job description.

THE TEACHING LOAD

The total, or effective teaching load, is a combination of several elements. These include the number of credits taught per semester (the absolute teaching load); the number of different course preparations; the number of contact hours with students in the classroom, laboratory, or studio; class size; and other non-classroom aspects of teaching duties such as advising students or holding study sessions. All contribute to the definition of and expectations for good teaching.

The Absolute Teaching Load

The absolute teaching load is obviously a definitive feature of any faculty position. Teaching is the primary duty of most faculty members, but teaching loads and the emphasis on teaching vary widely both between and within academic institutions and departments. How many classes or credits is your new faculty member expected to teach? You can be certain that this will be an important issue which candidates will consider when deciding whether or not to apply and which they will ask about during interviews. You must appreciate the extent to which the answer to this question determines the nature of the position and the degree to which it influences the choice of the best person to fill the job.

Your teaching load defines what good teaching means. Teaching 18 credits per semester at a junior college is a very different assignment from 3 credits per semester at a major research institution. A good choice for the former job will have very different expectations and abilities compared to the best candidate for the latter.

In choosing the best candidate for your position, you must carefully consider the absolute teaching load. For example, while persons with strong research credentials are often attractive candidates, these individuals may not be prepared to sacrifice the time they want to spend in the laboratory, library, or studio to teach the 12 credits per semester that they will be assigned. Rather than having a dissatisfied colleague who looks good on paper, you may be much happier with someone who expects and is willing to spend time on classroom-related duties. The persons you select will be more satisfied and more likely to stay and do a good job, if they are well-suited to the position. If your position involves less teaching and more scholarship or administrative activity, the same tenets apply.

Teaching Outside the Classroom

Part of any teaching load includes working with students outside the classroom. For example, does your department value collaborative scholarship with students as a means of promoting active learning or teaching science? If this is the case, you should include collaborative effort and time for this type of work in your expectations for, and description of, the position to be filled. Candidates who publish extensively but do not involve students in research would be a poor fit for such a position.

The Number of Different Course Preparations Required

Another teaching load consideration is the number of different course preparations the position requires. Fink (1984) studied geography professors' performance in their first year as faculty and found that "…it is not the number of classroom hours itself that creates problems for new teachers but rather the number of class preparations and the number of students involved" (p. 42). How many courses will be new preparations for the candidate? To expect someone to teach four courses, each with a different preparation, increases the effective teaching load. A higher teaching load (more credits/semester) with fewer course preparations and smaller classes may allow better teaching and an easier transition than fewer required credits with many different courses to prepare and teach.

The Number of Contact Hours With Students in the Classroom

Along the same line, how many contact hours will the candidate have? Some faculty in the sciences and fine arts have a teaching load which appears equal to their colleagues in other disciplines until one notes the number of hours they must spend with students in the laboratory or studio. These additional hours increase the effective teaching load.

Class Size

The number of students in courses is directly related to the effective teaching load. A faculty member with classes of 200 may cope by giving multiple choice examinations and having teaching assistants to help with study groups. But if classes used to be 30 students and now are 50 or 55, are faculty still expected to assign lengthy term papers, give essay examinations, and spend time with students as if these were "small" classes? Conversely, while honors or graduate classes of 10 or 15 may be intense in their intellectual focus and content, the collateral work of managing office hours, student questions, and reading assignments may be easier than for larger classes.

Level of Courses

The mix of graduate and undergraduate courses, and within undergraduate teaching, the mix of upper and lower division courses also affects the effective teaching load. Sometimes the load increases when faculty have responsibilities both in graduate and undergraduate programs. In other cases teaching is more difficult with intense graduate seminars, or high demand undergraduate classes may require the greatest effort.

Other Particulars of the Teaching Assignment

A final teaching load consideration is the circumstances under which the candidate will be teaching. A person with a teaching load of primarily freshmen-sophomore courses in a department with heavy needs in this area and many students to teach may experience a very heavy load. So might someone who teaches several large junior-senior classes per semester. Candidates applying for a position at a residential college may find a wider definition of what it means to participate and teach in the academic community than exists at other types of institutions. For example, they may be expected to participate in on-campus activities or to consider becoming a fellow of a dormitory.

NONTEACHING RESPONSIBILITIES

Those recruiting are well aware of the various nonteaching duties that are a part of the typical position. Candidates who are uninformed about the time faculty spend in professional activities other than teaching should be informed about such matters as early as possible in the recruiting process. Most faculty positions will require some professional activity such as artistic performance or research for tenure and promotion, and most new faculty welcome the opportunity to engage in such activity (and many new PhDs will be disappointed in the extent to which the time and facilities they were accustomed to in graduate school are not available to do so).

As with teaching load, specific institutions and faculty positions differ widely in their requirements of scholarship, or other nonteaching responsibilities, and the nature of such expectations also contributes to defining the nature of the position and the best candidate to fill it. In order to provide some structure to help you think about and describe the position you will be filling, we will use a simple two-dimensional model reflecting the magnitude of both the teaching and scholarly (artistic) expectations associated with a specific position. We begin with these two dimensions because the mix of teaching and scholarship "...comes close to determining everything else about academic life" (Clark, 1987, p. 263). This model can be useful not only in defining the position, but also in planning for recruitment and in the selection process. The following exercise may best be done individually, or by the recruitment committee as a whole, depending upon what will work best for those involved.

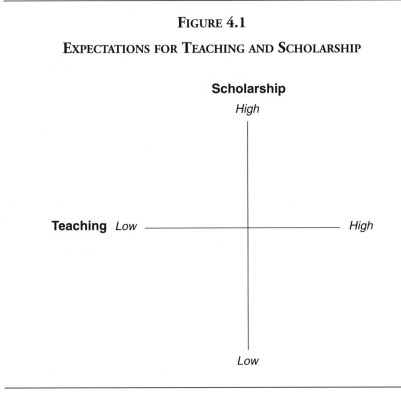

FIGURE 4.1

EXPECTATIONS FOR TEACHING AND SCHOLARSHIP

Scholarship
High

Teaching *Low* ———————|——————— *High*

Low

What is the Nature of Your Current Faculty/Department?

Place an "X" on the model in the location that best describes the activities of each of your colleagues. You now have a structural representation of your department regarding overall scholarly (artistic) and teaching activity.

Now insert a provisional "C" (Candidate) in the location describing your ideal expectations for the new hire. If there is a significant difference in location between the ideal which represents the desired behavior of the new faculty you are recruiting (let us say high in scholarship and high in teaching load), and the performance of individual faculty who already work in your department, you must consider whether it is realistic to expect what you do from the new hire. If the new person will be expected to do more than current faculty, assess the environmental supports for such activity.

What Are Institutional Expectations?

Now use this model to summarize your department and university activity. First, draw a circle or square around the area within which typical faculty activity and achievement fall within your department. Repeat this exercise for typical faculty activity within your institution. If there are noticeable differences between these two domains, then either your department has higher or different expectations than your institution, or vice versa. Either way, you will need to be aware of these differences in order to recruit the person best suited to perform in this environment. If faculty activity in your department is significantly less than for other faculty, you may need to consider other units' expectations as you hire, as faculty from other units are typically involved in setting contractual renewal and tenure thresholds for their institution and in evaluating faculty performance for renewal, tenure, and promotion.

Any gap between your department and others suggests the existence of a difference between your institutional culture, resources, or goals and those of the department. This gap is critical in that it may signal a divergence between institutional and departmental expectations, and both candidate and department need to understand the practical consequences of this situation so that they may be addressed, or at least accommodated.

What Needs Must Your Position Fill?

After you have looked at your curricular needs, the needs of your students, and the rough structuring of your department and institution by using this model, place an RC (Realistic Candidate) in your model in a location which realistically represents the type of person your program needs. This could be a high-high person, someone who works more at and wants to spend more time in teaching than scholarship, or vice versa.

If you have found the use of this model illuminating, you might extend the exercise with new sets of axes labeled teaching and service, or scholarship and service, or include any other important responsibility for your new colleague. The same principles apply.

In the end, you will want to integrate the results of this exercise into the position description and a workable set of selection criteria to be applied during your recruitment. Of course candidates can do self-assessments of their abilities, strengths, and interests, and assess jobs and departments in the same way.

PERCEPTION IS REALITY

We all know someone who is extremely productive and yet is always able to undertake another task when needed, while another person may seem to do little but complain about the unrealistic workload and the lack of time to complete assigned tasks. Whatever the actual workload, it may seem too demanding of teaching, scholarship, and/or service depending upon the experience, expectations, and needs of the individual in question. What constitutes a high workload for any of these areas is based in large part on how it feels to the faculty member. Teaching two courses a semester can seem like an incredibly difficult and stressful task if you are a new teacher, or if you are someone who has been teaching one course a semester, or one a year (especially if significant scholarship and service are also expected). To experienced teachers, or those now teaching 12 or more credits a semester, such a teaching load might seem like a sabbatical leave. Similarly, a regional university which for 100 years has required no published articles for tenure or promotion and now requires one may suddenly feel like a very high scholarship-demand environment.

Most new PhDs have been immersed in a high-demand research environment, often with some teaching as a means to earn extra income. When hired as faculty members, being given complete control of up to eight or more classes per year often comes on top of their existing, and usually unchanged, commitment to artistic performance or scholarship. Boice (1991, 1992), Getman (1992) and others have reported that new faculty members usually experience a reality shock during their first two years of work. They find themselves working as hard or harder as a new faculty member than they did in graduate school. Class preparation and teaching require unexpected amounts of time and energy.

When we talk about this unexpected hard work with doctoral students or faculty members just beginning their careers, we often encounter surprise, bewilderment, and/or disappointment. To avoid disillusionment, frustration, and dissatisfaction with academic life, a situation benefiting no one, help candidates develop realistic expectations of what faculty life entails as part of your recruitment process.

ORGANIZATIONAL CULTURE

Organizational and departmental culture are a primary determinant of faculty life. "Culture is an organization's basic beliefs and assumptions about what the organization is all about [and] how its members should behave..." (Cornwall & Perlman, 1990, p. 66). A culture shapes everything that happens in an organization and defines how things are done. In recruiting a good teaching faculty member, you need to determine what types of culture your organization and department have. Do they strongly support teaching, partially support it, give lip service to teaching, or ignore it altogether?

In a culture in which support, communication, and helping are positively valued, and one which has ongoing mentoring, a new faculty member with the potential for future teaching excellence would have an environment in which to grow and learn. In a culture in which faculty members fend for themselves, new hires with some previous faculty experience may be better able to survive and thrive. The recruitment committee should attempt to define a departmental or college culture to better articulate the experience level, coping skills, and other attributes expected of the candidates who will make up the pool of finalists. The same cultural issues apply to scholarship, artistic work, and other faculty responsibilities as well.

THE ISSUE OF FIT

Effective recruitment involves learning what needs to be done, the process and procedures, and then doing it. Included in this translation of particulars into practice is the relationship between the faculty position which you have now defined in some detail, candidate characteristics, and the nature of the fit between them. Bowen and Schuster (1986) have said that new appointees "commonly find themselves at institutions about which they know little or nothing and which they would have studiously avoided in a more favorable academic market" (p. 218). This is hardly an ideal situation. Maximizing the fit between position responsibilities and a candidate's interests and abilities requires that a recruitment committee has a clear perception of the nature of the job offered and the environment in which it exists, and that this information be communicated to the candidate. The committee must choose the person from the pool of candidates most able to do this particular job well over the long term.

It is easier to adjust the position before you hire someone than after you have failed to find a candidate well-suited to fill it. You may decide that good agreement between your position requirements and the skills and experiences of available candidates will be easier to achieve by modifying the nature of the position than by searching for the rare individual who could fit the demands of an unnecessarily difficult job. This modification may involve adjusting the responsibilities you expect the candidate to meet, the working environment, or the general context in which the job exists.

CHECKLIST

_____ Teaching expectations have been evaluated, including:

    _____ Absolute teaching load (# of credits)

    _____ Teaching outside the classroom

    _____ Number of different course preparations

    _____ Contact hours in the classroom or studio

    _____ Class sizes and expectations for how they are to be taught

    _____ Circumstances of teaching

_____ Amount of professional activity expected is determined.

_____ Other duties are identified.

_____ The unique nature of your position is defined including:

    _____ Understanding the nature of your faculty and department

    _____ Defining institutional expectations for faculty

    _____ Determining if what your department expects of new faculty is in the mainstream of your institutional expectations, more rigorous, or less

    _____ Synthesizing this information into the specific position you need

_____ Departmental and institutional cultures are understood.

_____ There is a strong possibility of a good fit between the position and candidates you will be evaluating.

EXERCISE

The scenario

Imagine (it should not be difficult) a regional university in transition for the past two decades. Faculty who were hired 20 years ago with the understanding that good teaching was the focus of their effort now work with newer colleagues hired with expectations for scholarship. While the emphasis on scholarship has increased in the past decade, there is now a renewed emphasis on good teaching. In brief, faculty are expected to do everything, do more of it, and do it well.

The department has been successful in hiring good young faculty but not necessarily in retaining them. Some have stayed and earned tenure, but others have left either burned out, their contract not renewed, or because the private sector seemed more attractive (equally hard work but greater income). The department has now been given permission to recruit in a subdisciplinary area in which it needs a faculty member, and a recruitment committee has been formed. Some planning took place to evaluate the curriculum and the strengths and weaknesses of the undergraduate major. Several job descriptions from previous searches were collected and a new one was written which includes high expectations for teaching, scholarship, and service. The recruitment committee feels well-prepared to begin its search.

- *What tasks have not been attended to?*
- *What risks does the recruitment committee undertake if it proceeds?*
- *If you served on this recruitment committee, what issues would you bring up at its next meeting?*

Some answers

When it met next, one member of the recruitment committee indicated that she felt that by asking new colleagues to be everything to everyone (students, colleagues, department and university renewal, and tenure review committees) the risk was high that these persons might not be able to achieve tenure or might choose to leave. While some members of the recruitment committee wanted to move ahead with the search, she convinced them to devote one meeting to this issue. After all, what was one more hour given the total time they would spend in recruiting, or in repeating the process if they made a poor hiring decision by selecting a candidate ill-suited to an unnecessarily difficult position?

In this meeting the faculty member pointed out that collaborative scholarship with undergraduates was gaining in importance within the department and institution, yet was not mentioned in the department's renewal and tenure criteria, which heavily emphasized publishing in middle-level or prestigious journals. She wondered if this state of affairs would not prove unfair to a new colleague, and motivate a new faculty to engage in scholarship not involving students.

The recruitment committee recognized that the teaching load of three courses per semester allowed for and expected collaborative work with students, that this expectation should be made known to candidates, and that the best fit between department needs and candidates would depend, in part, on this criterion.

The recruitment committee decided to include this expectation in the present recruitment. It realized that questions for candidates and selection criteria needed to change from emphasizing the number of publications expected in high level journals to include a focus on candidates' philosophies and skills regarding scholarship with students and the journals and forums in which this collaborative scholarship could become public domain. It also recommended that departmental guidelines for contractual renewal and tenure be rewritten to include collaborative scholarship with students and allow such work to substitute for some, but not all, publishing in jury-reviewed journals. Lastly, it was decided to sponsor a meeting within the college to talk with colleagues from other disciples about the present status of expectations for scholarship in general, and collaborative scholarship in particular, funds for such efforts, and to invite the dean to participate.

REFERENCES AND RECOMMENDED READINGS

Boice, R. (1991). New faculty as teachers. *Journal of Higher Education, 62,* 150-173.

Boice, R. (1992). *The new faculty member.* San Francisco, CA: Jossey-Bass.

Bowen, H. R., & Schuster, J. H. (1986). *American professors: A national resource imperiled.* New York, NY: Oxford University Press.

Clark, B. R., (1987). *The academic life: Small worlds, different worlds.* Princeton, NJ: Carnegie Foundation for the Advancement of Teaching.

Cornwall, J. R., & Perlman, B. (1990). *Organizational entrepreneurship,* Homewood, IL: Irwin.

Davidson, C.I., & Ambrose, S. A. (1994). *The new professor's handbook: A guide to teaching and research in engineering and science.* Bolton, MA: Anker.

Deal, T. E., & Kennedy, A. A. (1982). *Corporate cultures.* Reading, MA: Addison-Wesley.

Diamond, R. M. (1994). *Serving on promotion and tenure committees: A faculty guide.* Bolton, MA: Anker.

Diamond, R. M. (1995). *Preparing for promotion and tenure review: A faculty guide.* Bolton, MA: Anker.

Fink, L. D. (1984). *The first year of college teaching.* San Francisco, CA: Jossey-Bass.

Getman, J. (1992). *In the company of scholars: The struggle for the soul of higher education.* Austin, TX: University of Texas Press.

Gibson, G. W. (1992). *Good start: A guidebook for new faculty in liberal arts colleges.* Bolton, MA: Anker.

Schein, E. H. (1985). *Organizational culture and leadership.* San Francisco, CA: Jossey-Bass.

5

RECOGNIZING GOOD TEACHING

Try to recall the best teachers you ever had. What made their teaching so good? Were they especially well-organized, unusually knowledgeable about their subjects, enthusiastic, readily available to students, or did they have exceptional interpersonal skills? It was probably some combination of these, though you can see this is a difficult question to answer. It is even more difficult for a recruitment committee to determine if a candidate for a teaching position will teach well, given the limited information usually available to it.

The central qualities that make for successful teaching can be simply stated: command of the material to be taught, a contagious enthusiasm for the play of ideas, optimism about human potential, the involvement of one's students, and—not least—sensitivity, integrity, and warmth as a human being. When this combination is present in the classroom, the impact of a teacher can be powerful and enduring. (Boyer, 1987, p. 154)

THE NEED TO RECOGNIZE GOOD TEACHING

This chapter discusses the necessity of recognizing a good teacher, and presents three different approaches to help with this important recruitment task. Let us assume that you have assessed your department, corrected obvious problems, have considered the issues of context, perception and fit, and are now ready to hire and support a good teaching faculty member. How do you identify such individuals from among the various candidates who differ so much from one another, and from you, on how they approach students, pedagogy, and the classroom?

Recruitment committee members must be knowledgeable and sensitive enough to appreciate different areas and types of teaching excellence when assessing candidate teaching abilities and potential. An appreciation of varying teaching styles will ensure that important elements of good teaching are not overlooked, and that the most promising instructors are recognized. For these reasons, you should strive to be open to and appreciative of the various teaching styles and models you will encounter during the recruitment process.

Even if we are receptive to various approaches to teaching and knowledgeable regarding the diverse factors involved, we must still find ways to discover the extent to which each candidate possesses these characteristics and abilities. Therefore, as we discuss each definitional model of good teaching, we will provide a sample question or two you might ask candidates in order to elicit a discussion regarding their teaching. There are no right answers to these questions, but an intelligent response and discussion of questions such as these can be very useful in a recruitment committee's evaluation of a candidate, or a candidate's evaluation of a position.

GOOD TEACHING

The McFadden and Perlman Model

Susan McFadden and Barry Perlman (1989) have developed a model (see Figure 5.1) that identifies three basic elements (self-efficacy, interpersonal skills, and pedagogy) which contribute to teaching ability. Each element has three common underlying dimensions (intellectual, emotional, and moral) which further define the basic elements of good teaching. Recruiters should attend to each of these elements as they read teaching portfolio materials and letters of recommendation, and talk with and observe candidates teach. While no candidate may be articulate and excellent in all of the nine areas the model identifies, this model helps to identify characteristics you may want to evaluate.

Self-efficacy

A crucial personal variable in personality is our belief in our own self-efficacy, i.e., our feelings of competence to successfully do things. There is much empirical evidence tying our feelings of self-efficacy to successful behavior. For our purposes in recruiting, we want to know if candidates believe that they can teach effectively. Confidence and a sense of purpose based on experience are important ingredients possessed by all good teachers. You will remember that the model presents three underlying dimensions which are part of self-efficacy.

FIGURE 5.1

A MODEL OF TEACHING EXCELLENCE

| | Dimensions | | |
Elements	Intellectual	Emotional	Moral
Self-efficacy	Intellectual strengths and contributions	Ability to manage affect	Competence to resolve moral questions
Interpersonal Skills	Intellectual engagement and cooperation	Responses to emotional issues	Conduct with colleagues and students
Pedagogy	Integration of scholarship and teaching	Responses to the affect of teaching	Commitment to ethical conduct

Reprinted from McFadden, S., & Perlman, B. (1989). Faculty recruitment and excellent undergraduate teaching. *Teaching of Psychology, 16,* 195-198

Intellectual. Is part of this efficacy based on a good knowledge of subject matter and a growing knowledge of pedagogy?

Emotional. Do applicants believe they can succeed at the emotional side of teaching—whether this be excitement about the subject matter or liking students?

Moral. Does the candidate believe she is able to recognize and resolve ethical (moral) issues in teaching?

Question for candidates. What experiences support your belief that you are or will be an excellent teacher?

Interpersonal Skills

Teaching is communal, and we interact with our students and colleagues almost every day. When recruiting a good teacher, it is important to assess the nature of interpersonal skills and the way and ease with which candidates relate to others. Good teaching faculty have strong interpersonal skills and interact well with others. You need to decide if candidates will wear well. Will they get along with others and fit into the climate of collegiality you are striving to develop or maintain?

Intellectual. Can the candidate relate to others intellectually, discuss ideas, and accept differing viewpoints?

Emotional. Can the candidate establish rapport, relate to students appropriately in a large lecture hall and in one-on-one teaching or advising situations? For example, in studio work, rapport is a highly important factor for successful student learning. Does the candidate have the ability to work with students who have strong feelings about course and topical issues?

Moral. Is the candidate sensitive regarding ethical conduct with students both in and out of the classroom, and with colleagues?

Good interpersonal skills are essential, and the ability to deal appropriately with problem situations involving students or colleagues is often overlooked as an essential skill. Such abilities are important to teaching success— as we know from observing those who do not perform well in such circumstances. A reasonable level of compassion, a sense of ethics, an appropriate and discreet use of power (Markie, 1994), a sense of appropriate boundaries, and a diplomatic manner can go a long way toward successfully defusing the potentially unpleasant confrontations that occasionally occur with students or staff.

This is an area that can be explored during any telephone conversations with references. During campus visits, observe the candidates' answering of student questions during a lecture or master class, informal time with students and secretarial staff, and during interview situations. If these interactions raise questions or concerns, follow-up contacts with the candidate or references may be useful.

Questions for candidates. Do your interpersonal skills provide a foundation for good teaching? In what areas do you need to develop your interpersonal skills to be an even better teacher and colleague?

How would you proceed if a conflict arose with a more senior professor regarding the use of laboratory or studio equipment or space? What would be the first thing you would do?

Pedagogy

You are recruiting someone who is or has the potential to be an excellent teacher, and you want to be able to choose among candidates who will identify themselves as working members of an institution devoted to learning. They must also have a good knowledge of pedagogical issues or a willingness to obtain such knowledge.

Intellectual. What is the candidate's understanding of teaching? For example, does the candidate understand that she does not have to lecture all of the time? Has the candidate thought about when to lecture and when to use a more dialectic inquiry? Does the candidate encourage student problem solving when teaching in a one-on-one situation?

Emotional. How does the candidate respond to the emotions inherent in teaching? Can she cope with the down feelings following failed lectures or just not being *with it* on a given day? Can she cope with the continuous nature of teaching, one class endlessly following on another? What thoughts and feelings does the candidate have about these issues?

Moral. Lastly, significant moral issues permeate teaching. For example, does the candidate appreciate that moral issues are inherent in the act of teaching itself in terms of viewpoints presented or the acceptance or rejection of student ideas? Other moral issues in teaching include syllabi as contracts, exams, and grading.

Question for candidates. In your opinion, what are the major elements of good teaching?

Practical Teaching Activities

Another approach to identifying the elements of good teaching involves attending to the practical things teachers know and do that contribute to instructional success. These abilities should be evaluated when assessing candidates' teaching materials and during interviews. Candidates may not have experience in all eight of these categories nor have excelled in all, but they might be expected to be able to discuss them knowledgeably.

Course preparation. A good teacher must be able to manage course development and administration, including a number of practical activities basic to successful instruction. The ability to organize and manage a course is essential to presenting a well-structured educational experience in a manner suited to the abilities and expectations of the students, and to the nature of those academic programs of which the course is a component. Tasks with which the new teacher must successfully deal include:

- Setting appropriate goals and objectives

- Deciding on course content

- Setting course difficulty

- Designing the course and course policies

- Selecting course materials: text, readings, etc.

- Developing syllabi

- Preparing lectures/demonstrations/labs/lessons

- Developing tests and evaluation techniques

The reader may think of a variety of other tasks and skills to include in this list. It is the candidates' responsibility to provide evidence that they can successfully organize and teach a class, and it is the responsibility of the recruitment committee to evaluate this evidence, or seek it out if it is not provided.

Questions for candidates. *How would you decide what content or chapters to include or leave out of the introductory class in your discipline, or any course for that matter?*

What information should you include in a syllabus?

Classroom work. Once the course is designed and prepared, your new colleague must be able to perform well in the classroom. Such performance should include mastery of the following classroom activities:

- Motivating students to learn

- Building rapport and classroom climate

- Lecturing

- Leading discussions in class

- Conducting discussion groups or review sessions

- Giving classroom demonstrations

- Teaching in laboratory settings

- Teaching in the art or music studio

- Teaching the large class

- Handling difficult questions

- Dealing with problem situations

The recruitment committee should seek evidence of the ability to accomplish these tasks successfully, and the wise candidate will provide such evidence for the committee's consideration.

Question for candidates. *Do you structure your lectures to conclude with the end of each class period, or do you often continue them into the next class if needed? Why?*

Teaching in the laboratory or studio. Laboratory or studio teaching includes skills and abilities that differ, at least in degree, from those required in the more typical classroom setting, and a variety of other duties are typically associated with these teaching assignments. Candidates who will have such assignments need specialized knowledge and experience to teach well. Issues such as the following should be discussed with candidates, and their ability to deal with such issues should be included in your selection criteria:

- In music, knowledge of repertoire and teaching materials for various skill levels

- Purchase, use, and maintenance of facilities and equipment

- Care of laboratory animals

- Safety

- Legal requirements

These nuts and bolts activities may not seem closely related to teaching skills, but they provide a necessary foundation for successful laboratory and studio instruction. Care must be taken that the person chosen for the job can manage a laboratory or studio, do research, create art, or perform music, teach and direct student assignments and artistic productions in these settings, and stimulate and encourage such activities.

Question for candidates. *What skills are needed to teach well in the laboratory or studio setting as compared to a more typical classroom?*

Instructional technologies. As part of their teaching, candidates will need to be familiar with a continually changing variety of instructional technologies. Few will demonstrate mastery of all of the following, but they should indicate an interest in acquiring teaching skills in the use of:

- Videotapes/films

- Other audiovisual techniques

- Games, simulations, or case methods

- Computers and multimedia presentations

- Library services

A discussion of this category of instructional activity provides an excellent opportunity to describe current facilities and to discuss the probability of being granted budgetary authority to improve current holdings. The candidate may take this opportunity to indicate any special instructional technology needs or desires.

Questions for candidates. *What balance do you prefer between lecture and non-lecture experiences in your presentation of course material?*

What do you think are the strengths and weaknesses of these two method-ologies?

Teaching within a context. College courses differ in their placement within an overall program or institutional curriculum. The prerequisite courses required, and thus the general level of preparation of our students (e.g., in mathematics and the sciences, Perlman & McCann, 1993), may be less than we might desire. In order to reflect curricular expectations and/or student preparation, successful teachers must be able to alter the focus and content of a course depending on whether it is taught as part of a:

- Liberal arts curriculum

- Pre-professional major

- Graduate school preparatory track

- Technical training program

- Graduate program/curriculum

While we often know what we would like to teach in a given class and how we would like to teach it, we must often alter our approach to reflect the context within which the class is taught. The ability to make such alter-ations is a significant factor in teaching success, and you will want to know the degree to which a candidate possesses these skills. Unfortunately, this is not something that can be readily judged from credentials or from observa-tion of a single guest lecture. You may want to include this subject in your general discussion of teaching philosophy with each candidate, or candidates may wish to bring up the subject to better understand departmental expec-tation and practice regarding the courses to be taught by the new hire.

Question for candidates. *How would content and instructional goals differ between an undergraduate course for students who enroll to meet a gen-eral education requirement and the same course restricted to majors only, most of whom will seek graduate training and education?*

Teaching across the curriculum. Teaching provides a variety of oppor-tunities to include content beyond the formal course objectives, and refer-ences can often be appropriately made to subjects both within and beyond the boundaries of the discipline being taught. In preparing course content, many instructors find it useful to consider the extent to which they might appropriately include the teaching of:

- Science

- Mathematics

- Writing

- Critical thinking

- Ethics

- Cultural diversity

- History of the discipline

If all instructors reinforced basic skills and broadened students' experience by including such content, both our students and our instructional colleagues would benefit. In your discussions with candidates, listen for and ask about attitudes related to teaching across the curriculum. If done to reinforce and enrich the normal course content and assignments, this is another sign of a good teacher. Candidates may wish to ask about the existence of any institutional efforts, such as the typical writing across the curriculum programs, which support such instruction.

Question for candidates. *How would you include the teaching of critical thinking in an undergraduate course?*

Assessing student learning. The evaluation and assessment of student learning is an essential, though rarely popular, instructional component. The candidate should be prepared to deal with the various elements of student performance evaluation, including:

- Creating assignments: papers, presentations, examinations, artistic work or performances

- Grading initial paper drafts or rewrites

- Allowing rewriting of papers or revisions in art work

- Preparing and grading exams

- Grading applied practicum experience

- Penalties for late assignments

- Assigning grades and grade distributions

Activities such as these constitute an important segment of basic instructional activity. The growing interest in student assessment will ensure that this is an area of continuing importance, and the evaluation of candidates should include a discussion of their experience and preferences in this area. Institutions differ in their internal culture and expectations regarding evaluation practices, and candidates would be wise to ask about such practices during interviews.

Questions for candidates. How do you decide if examinations are cumulative in course content? Would your exams be cumulative? Why or why not?

How would you handle students who feel you graded them unfairly on a paper or other course assignment? Can you clearly explain your grading criteria?

Out-of-classroom work. Experienced college teachers know that a large portion of their teaching activity takes place outside the classroom. Many of these interactions involve opportunities to significantly influence the training and education of students, and candidates must be prepared to perform appropriately in these situations. This means they should have a good working knowledge of, and probably some practical experience with such subjects or activities as the following:

- Students' rights and responsibilities
- Ethics of student-faculty relations
- Holding office hours
- Advising/counseling students
- Collaborative scholarship with students
- Advising honorary societies or student clubs
- Use of available university services for students

Interactions with faculty outside of the classroom are important to student development. In many institutions the opportunity for students to collaborate in faculty research is an excellent way for faculty to teach and for students to prepare for graduate school and/or the job market, and is a means whereby faculty can find help with their scholarship. Both candidates and recruitment committees have an interest in making sure this subject is discussed during the interview.

Question for candidates. What experiences have you had with students outside the classroom that have emphasized the importance of this part of teaching?

Development: Becoming and Remaining a Good Teacher

As you recruit, you will often find yourself educating applicants about what is required to teach well and to survive in academe. For some, this will be a real eye opener. Candidates need to know what they are getting into when they decide to teach, and committees need to be sure that applicants understand the nature of the job they will undertake if they accept a faculty position.

As an example of something which may not be well-understood by applicants, some candidates must be told that becoming a good teacher is a long-term developmental process, not a simple or natural skill mastered within two or three years so attention can be turned toward scholarship, consulting, artistic performing, or other interests. We believe that candidates who are interested in and willing to pursue developmental opportunities, such as being mentored, and who understand the necessity of doing so, are much more likely to enjoy long-term teaching success. There are a variety of activities, both within and outside the classroom, which will help to develop teaching skills. Some readings on the professional development of faculty are included at the end of this chapter to provide additional information on this topic.

Classroom related teaching development. Becoming a good teacher involves a number of activities which will improve classroom instruction, including:

- Improving mastery of subject matter

- Improving awareness of ethical issues in teaching

- Talking with students and colleagues about one's teaching and classes

- Using student evaluations/opinions

- Videotaping teaching

- Being mentored as a teacher

- Co-teaching

- Developing at one's art or craft by attending master classes or taking advanced lessons

Engaging in these activities will help ensure continued attention to and development of the skills necessary to become and remain a good teacher. Candidates should seek information on the availability of such opportunities, and recruitment committees should take steps to inform themselves regarding such support, and to improve it if necessary. New faculty members should develop the habit of continuously working to improve their teaching skills at the beginning of their careers so this practice will continue through the years. Such efforts may constitute a good example for others currently serving on the faculty as well.

Question for candidates. *If you were to receive low student teaching evaluations/opinions in a course, how would you react or interpret this input, and what would you do in response?*

Teacher development and survival. Recruitment committees must work with their departments to create an environment which facilitates the development of good teaching in new colleagues and in themselves as well. New faculty members may need help in:

- Becoming committed to teaching
- Knowing what and where to read about teaching
- Maintaining collegiality with colleagues
- Understanding academic freedom as it relates to teaching
- Knowledge of grants/financial support for teaching
- Attendance at teaching workshops or forums
- Time/task management
- Stress management

Once again, you may find yourself in the position of educating a candidate or new hire in the survival skills necessary to prosper in academia. For example, even a suggestion that candidates read to improve their teaching may seem conventional, even dull. Yet reading is convenient, efficient, economical, requires no new skills, provides incentive to further reading and hence further development, and reading does improve instruction (Weimer, 1988). Weimer (1988) discusses reading as a means to improve teaching and provides essential sources on teaching, learning, and lively lectures. Candidates should have a real interest in the support available for their development as a teacher and would be wise to ask questions about the degree to which a new hire may expect it.

Question for candidates. *Where would you read about teaching?*

CHECKLIST

_____ Have reviewed and considered the various components of good teaching.

    _____ Conceptual elements and dimensions

    _____ Practical skills and activities

    _____ Development

_____ Committee members have an open mind toward different teaching styles and ideas.

_____ Prepared to initiate in-depth discussions of teaching with candidates.

_____ Included the relevant factors involved in good teaching in the selection criteria.

_____ Support is available for the continued development of teaching skills after the new colleague is hired.

EXERCISE

The scenario

Your recruitment committee is meeting to narrow the field of candidates to those with the best fit and credentials for a teaching position. One candidate is an excellent lecturer. A second candidate has a different teaching style, using multimedia presentations extensively in her classes. A third candidate's teaching statement and background emphasize the use of discussions in the classroom.

The candidates have done a good job of providing evidence that they teach well. The one who uses multimedia approaches to teaching has information in her teaching portfolio showing that her students have examination results equal to other course sections in which a more traditional lecture approach is used. The candidate who uses discussions extensively in class has a well thought out philosophy in his teaching statement supporting this approach, and provides outlines of course content he introduces during each of the class discussions. This content is similar to what others include in lectures. Finally, the candidate who primarily lectures has high teaching evaluations and strong letters of recommendation from references who have seen him teach.

In fact, each candidate has strong letters of recommendation, some teaching experience, and on other criteria is a good fit for the position. All show the ability to manage the tasks of teaching, and each demonstrates an interest in continued development and mentoring as a teacher. Nonetheless, each runs into strong opposition from someone on your recruitment committee. Most of the department faculty use a lecture format, and one of the recruiting faculty wants someone who has a different teaching style. The multimedia person's pedagogical style is attacked by another as being showy. Lastly, one member of the committee is very uncomfortable with the candidate who uses discussions extensively and is worried about what students actually learn.

- *What problems does this scenario raise for an effective recruitment?*

- *Will potentially good teachers be excluded from further consideration?*

- *How would you deal with this situation?*

Some answers

Since other selection criteria such as fit and the ability to function as a good department citizen are positive, the recruitment committee needs to focus on the ability or potential to teach well. Do the candidates provide information supportive of their good teaching? The answer is yes.

The Teaching Leader on the recruitment committee argues that all three meet definitions of good teaching. They differ primarily in their pedagogical approaches to the classroom. Acting on this information, and after discussion, the recruitment committee advances all of the candidates to the next round of consideration.

REFERENCES AND RECOMMENDED READINGS

Barzun, J. (1991). *Begin here*. Chicago, IL: The University of Chicago Press.

Boice, R. (1991). New faculty as teachers. *Journal of Higher Education, 62*, 150-173.

Boice, R. (1992). *The new faculty member*. San Francisco, CA: Jossey-Bass.

Boyer, E. L. (1987). *The undergraduate experience in America*. New York, NY: Harper & Row.

Brookfield, S. D. (1990). *The skillful teacher: On technique, trust, and responsiveness in the classroom*. San Francisco, CA: Jossey-Bass.

Clark, S. M., & Lewis, D. R. (Eds.). (1985). *Faculty vitality and institutional productivity: Critical perspectives for higher education*. New York, NY: Teachers College Press.

Davidson, C.I., & Ambrose, S. A. (1994). *The new professor's handbook: A guide to teaching and research in engineering and science*. Bolton, MA: Anker.

Davis, B. G. (1993). *Tools for teaching*. San Francisco, CA: Jossey-Bass.

Diamond, R. M., & Gray, P. (1987, January). *National study of teaching assistants (Tech. Rep.)*. Syracuse, NY: Syracuse University Center for Instructional Development.

Duffy, D. K., & Jones, J. W. (1995). *Teaching within the rhythms of the semester*. San Francisco, CA: Jossey-Bass.

Eble, K. E. (1976). *The craft of teaching*. San Francisco, CA: Jossey-Bass.

Eble, K. E., & McKeachie, W. J. (1985). *Improving undergraduate education through faculty development*. San Francisco, CA: Jossey-Bass.

Ericksen, S. (1984). *The essence of good teaching*. San Francisco, CA: Jossey-Bass.

Erickson, B. L., & Strommer, D. W. (1991). *Teaching college freshman*. San Francisco, CA: Jossey-Bass.

Flood, B. J., & Moll, J. K. (1990). *The professor business: A teaching primer for faculty*. Medford, NJ: Learned Information.

Fink, L. D. (1990). New faculty members: The professoriate of tomorrow. *Journal of Staff, Program, and Organization Development, 8*, 235-245.

Gaff, J. G. (1975). *Toward faculty renewal.* San Francisco, CA: Jossey-Bass.

Gibson, G. W. (1992). *Good start: A guidebook for new faculty in liberal arts colleges.* Bolton, MA: Anker.

Gullette, M. M. (Ed.). (1984). *The art and craft of teaching.* Cambridge, MA: Harvard University Press.

Keith-Spiegel, P., Wittig, A. R., Perkins, D. V., Balogh, D. W., & Whitley Jr., B. E. (1993). *The ethics of teaching: A casebook.* Muncie, IN: Ball State University.

Lambert, L., & Tice, S. (Eds.). (1993). *Preparing graduate students to teach.* Washington, DC: American Association for Higher Education.

Lowman, J. (1984). *Mastering the techniques of teaching.* San Francisco, CA: Jossey-Bass.

McFadden, S., & Perlman, B. (1989). Faculty recruitment and excellent undergraduate teaching. *Teaching of Psychology, 16,* 195-198.

McKeachie, W. J. (1994). *Teaching tips: Strategies, research, and theory for college and university teachers (9th ed.).* Lexington, MA: D.C. Heath.

Markie, P. J. (1994). *Professor's duties: Ethical issues in college teaching.* Lanham, MD: Rowman & Littlefield.

New Directions for Teaching and Learning. Quarterly journal. San Francisco, CA: Jossey-Bass.

Newble, D., & Cannon, R. (1989). *A handbook for teachers in universities and colleges: A guide to improving teaching methods.* New York, NY: St. Martin's Press.

Nyquist, J. D., Abbott, R. D., Wulff, D. H., & Sprague, J. (Eds.). (1991). *Preparing the professoriate of tomorrow to teach: Selected readings in TA training.* Dubuque, IA: Kendall/Hunt.

Perlman, B., & McCann, L. I. (1993). The place of mathematics and science in undergraduate psychology education. *Teaching of Psychology, 20,* 205-209.

Perlman, B., Gueths, J., & Weber, D. A. (1988). *The academic intrapreneur: Strategy, innovation, and management in higher education.* New York, NY: Praeger.

Professional and Organizational Development Network in Higher Education. (1984). *To improve the academy: Volume III.* Pittsburgh, PA: POD.

Schuster, J. H., Wheeler, D. W., et al. (Eds.). (1990). *Enhancing faculty careers: Strategies for development and renewal*. San Francisco, CA: Jossey-Bass.

Seldin, P., & Associates. (1995). *Improving college teaching*. Bolton, MA: Anker.

Van Note Chism, N. (Ed.). (1987). *Institutional responsibilities and responses in the employment and education of teaching assistants: Readings from a national conference*. Columbus, OH: The Ohio State University Center for Teaching Excellence.

Weimer, M. (1988). Reading your way to better teaching. *College Teaching,* 36(2), 48-53.

Weimer, M. (1990). *Improving college teaching: Strategies for developing instructional effectiveness*. San Francisco, CA: Jossey-Bass.

Wright, W. A. & Associates. (1995). *Teaching improvement practices: Successful strategies for higher education*. Bolton, MA: Anker.

Jossey-Bass has an excellent series on Higher Education and another series entitled *Key Resources*.

Sage Publications has a good series titled *Survival Skills for Scholars*.

Two journals which deal extensively with college teaching questions are:
College Teaching
American Association for Higher Education Bulletin

6

THE TEACHING PORTFOLIO

In all likelihood, the last time you recruited, some of the people writing letters of recommendation had not seen the candidate teach, and the resumes probably contained little information on teaching. How will you learn about the teaching skills of candidates for your new position? What information could candidates provide which would be helpful for you in your assessment?

Recruitment committees that make teaching ability a major selection criterion need to learn about the scope and quality of candidates' teaching experiences, skills, and future potential. Materials which document teaching experience should be specifically requested and then carefully evaluated. This compilation of teaching materials is called a teaching portfolio, and your indication that such material will be sought from all semifinalists signals candidates that teaching is a priority in your search.

Teaching portfolios document teaching effectiveness and provide a systematic record of teaching experiences and activities. The use of teaching portfolios is growing in importance in higher education, primarily as a means to assess the teaching of faculty already on the job. We propose the requirement of such portfolios for the selection process during recruitment, and suggest that the document be limited to five to seven pages.

Teaching portfolios, sometimes called teaching dossiers, are traditional in areas such as art or architecture where individuals must display examples of their work. While a teaching portfolio for job applications would probably not be as extensive as Seldin's (1991, 1993) examples for established faculty, his books provide many useful ideas and suggestions. Your college or university faculty handbook also may have excellent ideas on descriptions of teaching and its presentation formats (required or recommended at your institution for personnel decisions).

Asking for a portfolio including experience, teaching philosophy, and course documents provides basic material for use in assessing candidates. The point is not necessarily that portfolios make it relatively easy to detect individuals who do not teach well, but that a teaching portfolio documents "…the complexity and individuality of good teaching" (Seldin, 1991, p. xi). Reading them permits you to differentiate among candidates, highlighting the different strengths of each and allowing a more accurate selection of the candidate whose skills and abilities are best suited to the unique nature of your position. They also increase the importance of teaching in a recruitment by complimenting the lengthy documentation usually presented to describe scholarship and current artistic performing or research interests (Seldin, 1991). The portfolio is to teaching what lists of grants, publications, and presentations are to scholarship.

Portfolios allow faculty to identify strengths and relative weaknesses in their teaching and force them to think about what it is they do and want to do when they teach. Many candidates will profit from preparing this material as they talk with others about teaching and consider their personal experiences.

USE OF A TEACHING PORTFOLIO

Require a Teaching Statement

We advise that all applicants be required to submit an initial one or two page statement addressing their teaching philosophy, goals, and other specific items in your selection criteria. The complete position description and briefer job announcement should include this brief teaching statement as a requirement for application.

Requiring a Teaching Portfolio

Make sure the recruitment committee talks with the department and dean about using a teaching portfolio as part of selection. Other colleagues and administrators may need to be apprised of the rationale behind this requirement, and of its enormous value in recruiting.

We recommend that complete portfolios be required only after the number of candidates has been sufficiently reduced to allow the recruitment committee to give each file a careful reading. For example, in a recruitment with 500 applications it makes no sense to read teaching portfolios from each candidate. After passes through the candidate files, including a careful reading of teaching statements, the remaining candidates should be asked to submit a complete teaching portfolio. This could be five candidates or 25, whatever the size of your pool of semi-finalists. If you know you will have only a few applicants for a specialized position, have all candidates who meet requirements for the position submit portfolios as early as possible.

Some candidates may not apply for your position, or they may withdraw, if teaching statements and portfolios are required. One result may be that only candidates interested in teaching will apply, and you will not have to process the credentials of those less suited to your position. However, requiring a teaching portfolio is not a threshold so high that desirable candidates will be discouraged from applying. It simply makes sense that in hiring a new faculty with teaching responsibilities you insist on information related to teaching for use in making your decision.

Candidates should note that the preparation of a teaching statement and/or portfolio for any one position will result in its availability for submission with any subsequent application and is to their potential benefit. This document can become the basis for the teaching information which new hires will be expected to prepare for performance reviews and personnel actions. Preparing this portfolio is not a waste of time.

Make Teaching Portfolios Useful and Relevant for Recruitment

Recruitment committees need to define the unique teaching position to be filled (see Chapters 3 and 4). Decide what teaching abilities and experiences are most important as selection criteria, and then request portfolios with information ordered from the most important criterion to the least (Seldin, 1991, 1993). This structure will fit the portfolio to your search and will greatly simplify the reading of teaching portfolios. It will also assist candidates in deciding whether they are a good fit for the opening and whether they want to apply.

Another approach is to require certain items and let candidates provide any other materials they wish (Seldin, 1993). For example, you could require (1) a teaching philosophy and goals statement, (2) documentation of past teaching experience, and (3) course syllabi, and then let candidates elect other materials to submit. What you require and leave as elective and secondary will depend on the characteristics of the position to be filled and on the nature of your selection criteria.

Limit Portfolio Length

No rational recruitment committee would ask for all of the information listed below. The amount of material would be overwhelming to candidates and recruiters alike and, therefore, of little use. A teaching portfolio used for recruitment need not be exhaustive, and after reviewing what the position requires, you will know how much of the following information will be useful. We concur with Seldin's (1991) recommendation that a teaching portfolio be limited to five to seven pages (plus appendices). Candidates should be concise and focused in what they say; recruitment committees in what information they request or require. Portfolio appendices can present a variety of teaching materials such as syllabi or student course evaluations/opinions. Table 6.1 outlines teaching portfolio content.

Ask for Self-Evaluation Statements

For each major area of information, we suggest you request a brief self-evaluation. If you want a more extensive self-evaluation you can suggest some of the major areas in Table 6.1 as themes.

Write a Teaching Portfolio Description

When you have arrived at consensus on what you want in submitted teaching portfolios, write a one page description of these materials. This description can be provided to candidates who apply, along with your letter of acknowledgement of their application, informing them that all semi-finalists will be asked to submit one and recommending they begin work on writing their teaching portfolio.

MAJOR AREAS IN A TEACHING PORTFOLIO

The teaching portfolio's basic structure calls for (1) a concise reflective narrative that includes selective information as outlined by the criteria determined by the nature of your position, and (2) an appendix of the hard copy documentary evidence (e.g., syllabi, examinations). The portfolio should not be a vast compilation of reflection and materials, but is instead a concise and analytical self-evaluation.

Candidate Statement on Teaching

Teaching philosophy, strategy, goals, and rewards. This statement should be required from all candidates. As an integral part of a teaching portfolio for recruitment purposes, the candidate statement speaks to teaching philosophy, strategies, goals, successes, failures, and future work. Ask new PhDs what they learned from TA training, teaching seminars, or past teaching. The statement can contain content on any area important to the recruitment committee. Be sure to ask what rewards candidates receive from teaching and what is satisfying for them. In brief, why do they want to teach?

TABLE 6.1

TEACHING PORTFOLIO INFORMATION

1. Candidate Statement on Teaching
   - Philosophy
   - Strategies
   - Goals
   - Rewards

2. Depth, Breadth, and Expertise in Teaching
   - Specialty area and courses a candidate could teach in this area
   - Breadth, other areas and courses a candidate feels prepared to teach
   - Self-Evaluation

3. Teacher Preparation and Experience
   - Past Teaching including Teaching Assistant experience
   - Information and Observations on courses taught
   - Teaching Innovations
   - Self-Evaluation

4. Instructional Materials and Feedback
   - Course Syllabi, Reading or Repertoire Lists From Courses Taught
   - Student Evaluations/Opinion Data
   - Peer Evaluations of Teaching
   - Examinations and Assignments
   - Teaching Technology and Equipment Needed
   - Work With Students Outside the Classroom or Studio
   - Outcomes of Teaching (e.g., student posters, papers, recitals)
   - Teaching Across the Curriculum
   - Awards/Recognition
   - Videotape of Teaching or Artistic Performance, Presentation of Art Work
   - Self-Evaluation

5. Development as a Teacher
   - Reading
   - Other Evidence of Development
   - Self-Statement

The authors evaluated the teaching statements requested of candidates applying for an assistant professor, undergraduate teaching position (Perlman, Marxen, McFadden, & McCann, in press) and found that applicants presented little teaching information in requested teaching statements and did not emphasize teaching experience or present teaching credentials well. Conversations with these and other candidates revealed that many had never reflected on what it is they do when they teach, nor had they systematically written about their teaching philosophy and goals. Since the information available in candidate teaching statements may be limited, recruitment committees should ask for the other teaching portfolio information detailed in this chapter. Applicants usually anticipate greater interest in other aspects of their credentials (e.g., scholarship).

Customizing the teaching statement. The teaching statement can be customized to fit the specific needs and responsibilities of each position to be filled. If you are interested in studio teaching, ask each candidate to address this pedagogical issue. If you want to know about candidates' awareness of ethical issues in teaching, ask them to write about this topic.

Depth, Breadth, and Expertise

Specialty area. Ask candidates to describe their specialty area, list courses they can teach in this area, and provide a statement on expertise in this subject matter.

Breadth. Many departments, especially at smaller institutions, need faculty who can teach a wide variety of courses in different subareas of a discipline or in multidisciplinary courses. Ask candidates to indicate all courses they feel prepared to teach; i.e., what is the degree of their preparation and knowledge in non-specialty areas, and what are they willing to learn about? In many colleges flexibility and intellectual breadth are desirable attributes.

Self-evaluation of depth, breadth, and expertise. Ask for a brief statement on how and why candidates became expert in their areas of competence. If depth is a strength, have them describe the depth of their knowledge and work. If they have breadth, why is this?

Teacher Preparation and Experience

Past teaching. Past teaching may have taken place in a wide variety of institutions including high school or adult education. College teaching is common, often as a teaching assistant (TA).

TA experience. You may want to ask specific questions about TA experience since it can vary from supervising study groups and writing examinations to sole responsibility for a course, from required teaching seminars and extensive supervision to the sink or swim experience many of us remember. Information on the following components of a candidate's TA training experience may be useful (Mueller, Perlman, McFadden, & McCann, 1996): (1) faculty supervision; (2) components of TA training (e.g., seminars, workshops, use of handbooks, observation); (3) specific TA instruction (e.g., the process of teaching, ethics, text selection, writing syllabi, lecturing); (4) the value of teaching in the department and TA program; (5) level at which training was provided (e.g., department, university, or both); (6) was training required, recommended or neither; (7) what was learned about working as a faculty and about higher education; and (8) areas of teaching responsibility and actual teaching tasks performed (e.g., lecture, prepare exams, lead study groups, supervise labs, teaching a course).

Information and observations on courses taught. You will want a list of courses taught with sole responsibility, team taught, or assisted as a TA. For each course, request its number of credits and enrollment. Candidates can be asked to comment on the course philosophy and goals, class size, what they would do differently next time, course constraints (e.g., large size class with no TAs; antiquated or absence of up-to-date musical, art, or scientific equipment), and so forth. What was the nature of the students taught, and what effort was made to teach these students well? Ask about participation in developing new courses or in major course revisions. Have candidates developed materials such as course manuals, audio-visual support, or study guides? If so, ask for a description of them. Candidates may be asked to submit these materials if they are important to your search.

Teaching innovations. Candidates may be asked to describe alternative delivery systems they have tried, or other innovations. For example, specific attention may be paid to distance learning if such instruction will be required. If efforts to incorporate materials and methods which address issues of diversity are needed, ask about such experiences. Determine if the candidate can teach a mainstream course in a normal fashion. No amount of alternative instruction can make up for a lack of traditional teaching skills.

Self-evaluation of teaching preparation and experience. Candidates can present a self-evaluation of their course planning and preparation. Recruitment committees should assess these teaching materials on several dimensions, such as how courses are taught, the load, number of new preparations, or if extensive traveling to teach was necessary.

Instructional Materials and Feedback

Course syllabi and reading lists. Ask experienced candidates to submit select course syllabi from different types of courses (graduate or undergraduate, small seminar or large auditorium). New PhDs with limited teaching experience may only have one or two available. In reading syllabi, note if they offer the basic information you expect. Put yourself in the student's place and decide how clear the syllabus is and how approachable or distant the instructor seems. Look through reading lists for a sense the candidate is aware of classics in an area and insight into candidates' interests outside their discipline.

Student evaluations and opinions. For someone who has been teaching full-time for a year or two, course evaluations from all courses are not necessary; ask for one graduate and one undergraduate, or evaluations from a large class and a seminar or studio class. If your committee is interested, let the candidate know that select written student comments may be included. Of course candidates may send only their best efforts, so keep this in mind when you read them. Some candidates may submit letters or other evidence of student satisfaction with teaching as well.

Peer evaluations of teaching. Peer evaluations of teaching often provide detailed pictures of a candidate's teaching. Classroom or studio visits are the most valuable. At times this content may be included in letters of recommendation. Other peer evaluations may speak to contributions to the department's curriculum and major programs of study.

Examinations, assignments, and major projects. Ask for examinations and other course assignments from different types of courses. Attend to the quality of the exam items used and whether they assess the subdiscipline information you believe students should be learning. Do the examinations seem clearly worded and fair, neither too easy nor tremendously difficult? You may want to ask candidates what types of grading they use—cumulative points or does each exam yield a letter grade? Why does the candidate grade that way? What distribution of grades does a candidate typically give in each course and why? Do not mistake unrealistic expectations for rigor.

If candidates require term papers or other writing, what type of feedback do they provide? Do they pre-read, meet with students individually, or ask for a reference list or an outline before the paper is written?

Teaching technology and equipment needed. Ask candidates to provide a list of equipment they absolutely need to teach certain classes, and any technology and equipment that would be desirable, but is not essential. These requests not only tell you something about their teaching but also about the fit between what they need to teach well and what technology exists to support teaching in your department and institution.

Awards and recognition. Candidates should be asked to list any teaching awards or other special recognition.

Work with students outside the classroom. Commitment to teaching will be evident in candidates' teaching statements, but you may want to ask if they have worked with students collaboratively in independent study, related readings, recital preparation, senior theses, master's theses, or dissertations. Have they advised a departmental club or honorary society? In other words, has the candidate shown a liking for students and a commitment to working with them outside the classroom? Such evidence tells a lot about a candidate's relationship with students.

Outcomes. Ask candidates to submit student work they supervised, such as posters presented at state or regional conferences, a student performance in music or theater, papers written, practicum evaluations, or other evidence. New PhDs may have few of these. Another outcome is student decisions about work and graduate school. Student statements about influencing graduate education, choice of a career or major yield insights into candidate teaching and advising.

Teaching across the curriculum. Many faculty members teach beyond the discipline in their classes. Ask if they do teach any content or skills across the curriculum such as writing, science, math, ethics, or diversity. They should describe how they became interested in this area and how and why they teach it.

Videotape of teaching or performing, presentation of art work. Require that finalists for a position submit a videotape of teaching or performing prior to campus visits. This videotape should cover at least 50 minutes to an hour of a class, studio, or laboratory. Such a submission is a common part of a candidate's application in the fine arts. Again, candidates will submit tapes of their best effort. These bring the candidates to life for a recruitment committee and provide a good idea of the teaching ability and potential of each finalist. We have heard of at least one search which used such videotapes to determine the ethnicity and appearance of candidates. Such uses are illegal and unethical.

Self-evaluation of teaching. Some of the self-evaluative statements for this section may be found in the teaching statement required of all applicants. But you can ask candidates how they learned to write syllabi, what they think of and how they respond to their student evaluations, and/or what they would do differently the next time they teach a course.

Development as a Teacher

Reading. Some new PhDs will not be fully aware that good teaching is a developmental process, and you will help them discover this fact by asking for information on how they have developed as a teacher. Candidates will start to think about teaching if asked not only what teaching literature they read, but what is the best article or book they have read in the past six months, and why. What would they recommend you read about teaching, and what is the best source of teaching tips in the discipline they have discovered?

Other evidence of development. Activities such as mentoring other faculty or TAs, or other improvement of instruction assignments should be detailed. If candidates report attending conferences or workshops, ask what they learned about teaching. In the fine arts it is important to ask about lessons, performing, directing, or exhibitions.

Self statement on development. Ask candidates who has been the biggest influence on their motivation to teach and why, or if they are better teachers now than one or three years ago and how they are better. What teaching changes are they planning for the next year or two? How much time do they spend keeping current with content and pedagogy, and how do they do so?

ASSESSING TEACHING PORTFOLIOS

The following recommendations on assessing teaching portfolios are based on our own experiences and those of others, including Seldin (1993).

Be Systematic

If the recruitment committee has done its planning and preparatory work (see Chapters 3 to 5), the position will be defined in some detail, and the specific elements of good teaching most desirable in candidates will be identified. These can be summarized in a teaching portfolio rating sheet for each recruitment committee member. An example of such a portfolio rating form is presented in Table 6.2. The *Other Important Criteria* section contains criteria based on the latest recruitment in our department. You would insert *Other Important Criteria* as appropriate.

The more systematic the reading of the portfolios, the greater the likelihood of accurate, reliable, and good decisions. Label topics required in all portfolios as core areas. Leave space for remarks and ratings of optional areas and for comments. You may want an overall ranking on the entire portfolio and/or separate rankings on each of the major areas. Several models for evaluating portfolios are listed in Seldin (1993). We strongly advise that you restrict your evaluation sheet to one side of one page.

TABLE 6.2

AN EXAMPLE OF A TEACHING PORTFOLIO RATING FORM

Candidate Name_____

Complete Portfolio   Yes   No

	Poor	Fair	Good	Very Good	Excellent
Core Areas					
Candidate Teaching Statement	1	2	3	4	5
Depth and Expertise	1	2	3	4	5
Breadth	1	2	3	4	5
Teacher Preparation and Experience	1	2	3	4	5
Instructional Materials and Feedback	1	2	3	4	5
Development as a Teacher	1	2	3	4	5
Other Important Criteria					
Instructional Activity Outside the Classroom	1	2	3	4	5
Overall Ratings					
Fit for Position	1	2	3	4	5
Teaching Abilities and Potential	1	2	3	4	5

Remarks—Other Information Needed

Perlman, Baron, & McCann, Lee I. (1996). *Recruiting good college faculty: Practical advice for a successful search.* Bolton, MA: Anker.

Ask Candidates to Attend Carefully to Portfolio Content and Format Requirements

Candidates will expend effort in preparing a portfolio, and you want this time to be productive both for them and for your committee. It is our experience that candidates often do not tailor their credentials to a specific position (Perlman, Marxen, McFadden, & McCann, in press). Make sure that candidates know the expected length, content areas, and format of the portfolio. Be clear about what is required information and what is optional, if anything. If portfolios are similar in format, it is easier to focus on their content and the differences between candidates.

Be Aware of Candidate Experience Level

One dimension to keep in mind is the experience level of candidates. Experienced candidates have taught more, and their teaching portfolios may be fuller and on occasion more polished and thoughtful. In reading information provided by relatively new faculty, keep in mind that they lack experience and look for good ideas, good writing, and maturity. Remember that each of the faculty on a recruitment committee was young once, and that excellent teaching is a developmental process.

Use Multiple Sources of Teaching Information

Keep your position criteria clearly in mind when evaluating teaching and do not use the teaching portfolio alone. Always expect to have to follow up to obtain more information on teaching for a certain number of candidates. Be sure to talk with candidates on the phone or during visits about teaching and watch them teach when they visit your campus. Do not base decisions on one entry in the portfolio. One very high rating is not sufficient. Look for a good fit with the most important areas for the position you are filling throughout the teaching portfolio and other application materials.

Read for Writing Style and Content

In reading teaching portfolios, you will encounter varying uses of language and writing styles. These provide a variety of useful information about candidates' attitudes, expectations, priorities, and approaches to teaching and students.

Teaching Statements May Disappoint You

As noted (Perlman, Marxen, McFadden, & McCann, in press), few candidates will write first-rate teaching statements, so read them within this context. After reading the first five or 10, you may have to reread earlier statements and adjust your evaluations. However, the lack of robust teaching statements by faculty candidates should not be taken as evidence of a lack of commitment to teaching. In a study of the faculty teaching role for new faculty, we looked at 59 new psychology faculty, each working in a different institution, and found a great interest in and commitment to teaching (Perlman, Konop, McFadden, & McCann, 1996).

CHECKLIST

_____ Recruitment committee members have seen teaching portfolios (read Seldin, 1991, 1993).

_____ A decision is made on whether a teaching portfolio will be part of this recruitment.

_____ Department and dean approve use of a teaching portfolio.

_____ Information you want candidates to supply is determined.

_____ Desired teaching information is prioritized: candidates will write portfolios with the most important information first.

_____ Criteria for assessing teaching portfolios are selected.

_____ One page rating form to facilitate a systematic, reliable reading of portfolios is created.

_____ Issues involved in evaluating portfolios are reviewed.

EXERCISE

Rather than presenting information, raising questions, and providing some answers, this exercise asks you to do something different. Write down some ideas as preparation for writing your own statement on teaching covering such topics as teaching philosophy, strategies, goals, and the rewards of teaching. Now take each of the next four major sections in a teaching portfolio (breadth, depth, and experience; teacher preparation and experience; instructional materials and feedback; and development as a teacher) and jot some notes on your own teaching as a beginning or outline for your own statement in each category.

As you progress, keep track of what it is you do well as a teacher and what it is, perhaps after many years, with which you still struggle. Where has your teaching gotten better, and how long did it take to finally teach that introductory course or advanced seminar the way you really wanted?

Make a list of personal characteristics which enhance and contribute to good teaching, and those which detract from your classroom or studio goals. Next, look at your course syllabi. How many could be improved? Do the same for your examinations and assignments.

Finally, take the rating form example (Table 6.2) and rate yourself. How would you fare as a candidate for your department's next vacant position?

We hope this exercise helps you realize the developmental possibilities in creating a teaching portfolio. Do you now have a sense of how portfolio materials help you differentiate between candidates and of the work involved to prepare one?

REFERENCES AND RECOMMENDED READINGS

Centra, J. A. (1994). The use of the teaching portfolio and student evaluations for summative evaluation. *Journal of Higher Education, 65*, 555-570.

Diamond, R. M. (1995). *Preparing for promotion and tenure review: A faculty guide*. Bolton, MA: Anker.

Diamond, R. M. (1994). *Serving on promotion and tenure committees: A faculty guide*. Bolton, MA: Anker.

Edgerton, R., Hutchings, P., & Quinlan, K. (1991). *The teaching portfolio: Capturing the scholarship in teaching*. Washington, DC: American Association for Higher Education.

McFadden, S., & Perlman, B. (1989). Faculty recruitment and excellent undergraduate teaching. *Teaching of Psychology, 16*, 195-198.

Mueller, A., Perlman, B., McCann, L. I., & McFadden, S. (1996, January). *Teaching assistant training in psychology—1994 study*. Poster presented at the 18th Annual Institute for the Teaching of Psychology, St. Petersburg Beach, FL.

Perlman, B., Konop, K., McFadden, S., & McCann, L. I. (1996, January). *A study of the faculty teaching role*. Poster presented at the 18th Annual Institute for the Teaching of Psychology, St. Petersburg Beach, FL.

Perlman, B., Marxen, J. C., McFadden, S., & McCann, L. I. (in press). Applicants for a faculty position do not emphasize teaching. *Teaching of Psychology*.

Seldin, P. (1991). *The teaching portfolio: A practical guide to improved performance and promotion/tenure decisions.* Bolton, MA: Anker.

Seldin, P., & Associates. (1993). *Successful use of teaching portfolios.* Bolton, MA: Anker.

Seldin, P., & Associates. (1995). *Improving college teaching.* Bolton, MA: Anker.

Shore, M. B., and others. (1986). *The teaching dossier (rev. ed.).* Montreal, Quebec: Canadian Association of University Teachers.

Wright, W. A., & Associates. (1995). *Teaching improvement practices: Successful strategies for higher education.* Bolton, MA: Anker.

EVALUATING SCHOLARSHIP AND ARTISTIC PERFORMANCE

What is the place of scholarship or artistic performance in your curriculum, department, and institution? What forms of scholarship are expected and/or acceptable? How will you assess candidates' abilities and potential to meet these expectations?

Most faculty are expected to do more than teach. While the focus of this book is on recruiting good teaching faculty, we realize that you will probably expect scholarship and/or artistic performance and "service" activities as well. In subsequent chapters we will continue to emphasize teaching, but the same thinking and processes apply to scholarship. These include candid and open discussion between recruitment committee members, and including scholarship as a selection criterion in your position description and job announcement, screening of applicants, assessment during the campus visit, and choosing whom to offer a contract. Throughout this chapter the term scholarship also applies to expectations in the fine arts for creative achievement as a performing artist, or by appearance of work in juried exhibitions.

PLANNING: IDENTIFYING SCHOLARSHIP NEEDS AND EXPECTATIONS

No matter how superb the teaching of your new hires, if they cannot meet scholarship expectations they will probably not be retained. Recruitment committees must search for someone who can meet all of the criteria for contractual renewal and tenure, including both teaching and scholarship. To do this, you need to know what types of scholarship you want in a new hire and how that scholarship dovetails with the needs of your curriculum and students. These preferences can then be clearly stated in position descriptions and job announcements, in selection criteria, in letters to writers of letters of recommendation, and in discussions with candidates during telephone calls and campus visits. A clear idea of the preferred types of scholarship allows you to do a better job of screening candidates, allows candidates to assess how well their abilities and scholarly interests fit your position, and increases the chances of retention and tenure.

The Milieu in Which Scholarship Exists

A recruitment committee needs to develop specific selection criteria for scholarship just as it does for teaching, to provide a framework for the subsequent assessment of applicants' scholarly abilities and potential. Planning (see Chapter 3), which includes a discussion of nonteaching faculty responsibilities (see Chapter 4) should assess the milieu into which new hires are brought, including the role of scholarship or artistic performance in your department and institution.

In some institutions, often regional universities, upward drift (Boyer, 1990) is occurring as definitions of scholarship and productivity levels are changed to emulate those found in major universities. Some candidates, who consider scholarship important only in obtaining positions in major research universities, may be surprised to learn of the extent of such responsibilities in many regional universities and liberal arts colleges. Warch's (1992) statement on the place of scholarship in meeting the aims of liberal arts education shows that even small colleges emphasize collaborative scholarship between faculty members and students, and that they will look closely at candidates' scholarship credentials.

Simply put: Is yours a department and institution where teaching is a faculty's main responsibility, where teaching and scholarship are relatively evenly balanced, or where scholarship predominates (Gibson, 1992)? Evaluate the scholarship expected of new hires during planning. For example:

Quantity. Do new hires need two or three total publications to earn tenure or two or three a year?

Quality. Must publications be jury reviewed in middle- or upper-level journals, or is any publishing acceptable? Can scholarship be presented at regional conferences, or are only national meetings acceptable?

Time. How much time can new hires spend on scholarship? How available must they be to students for activities such as collaborative scholarship, office hours, or advising?

To further assess the milieu for scholarship a SWOT analysis (Chapter 3) of scholarship in your department and university may be helpful. Your strengths and opportunities may be more applicable to some types of scholarship than others, while identifying the weaknesses and threats, whether specific to certain types of scholarship or generalizable to all scholarly inquiry, will help the department begin changes to ensure that expectations more closely match reality.

What Types of Scholarship Do You Want?

Boyer's (1990) four-part taxonomy of scholarship provides a conceptual base for defining the types of scholarship which will best fit your department's curricular and student needs, and your institution's standards.

Scholarship as discovery. This is what most academics mean when they speak of "research." Discovery involves commitment to investigation for its own sake—pure research if you will. Many would argue that this type of scholarship defines what it means to be an academic.

Scholarship of integration. This type of scholarship makes connections between and across disciplines. It is interdisciplinary or intradisciplinary in nature. These scholars bring new explanatory models and insight to existing knowledge and give meaning and context to pure research.

Scholarship of application. Application scholarship applies knowledge to problems and assesses outcomes. This type of scholarship is the basis for land grant universities, and it emphasizes usefulness, with societal problems and situations as a research agenda. As Boyer (1990) points out, this is rigorous scholarly work. Some of university faculty's most widely known and appreciated work comes from this domain, whether it be medical applications or agriculture.

Scholarship of teaching. This scholarship studies teaching and makes it understandable to others. Boyer seems to say that teaching itself could be defined as a form of scholarship.

The Relationship of Scholarship to Your Curriculum

Regardless of the types of scholarship or artistic activity desired, another question to be asked is what forms this scholarship should take to best meet student needs and maintain or strengthen the curriculum. Take a step back and consider the contributions scholarship makes to your curriculum and in what courses and for which students it is most important. Do you want student research in a group setting in a laboratory (common with undergraduates) or supervised individually (oftentimes graduate students and some undergraduates)? If faculty work with doctoral students is valued, you need a new hire whose scholarship supports such research projects.

Other questions should be asked as well. Will ideal candidates need more than one area of scholarly interest or research to best meet student or programmatic needs? With how many students do you hope the new faculty can work? Is including one or two students acceptable, or does the department want a larger research team comprised of graduate students, undergraduates, or both? Departments should decide if they want an individual with a research program, that is, several related ideas or hypotheses to be tested, or someone with a more scatter-shot approach of conducting research on whatever seems interesting to students at the time. Both are valid methods of inquiry depending on departmental needs. If consensus on the definition and curricular goals of scholarship is reached before candidate files are read, better decisions will be made in selecting new hires.

EVALUATING CANDIDATES' ABILITIES AND ACHIEVEMENT

The prestige of a doctoral program or mentor is a popular, albeit inferior predictor of future research productivity (Thompson & Zumeta, 1985). These may be useful pieces of information, but you will want additional measures of scholarly ability and potential.

The Vitae

It is now common for new doctoral candidates to have public domain scholarship or artistic performance, and a vitae will typically provide information on scholarly presentations and journal articles published. Were these forums jury reviewed, was work submitted by request, or were all submissions accepted? Look for collaborative work with colleagues and for the order of authorship to indicate degree of responsibility for the scholarship.

Another useful piece of information is research assistant experiences. Working for different researchers in different laboratory or scholarly settings can enhance the ability of new hires to be independent scholars and increase their breadth and subsequent ability to work collaboratively with students.

Research Statement

We recommend requiring a statement on research or artistic performance as part of the initial application, just as one is required on teaching. But again, do not assume that if you ask you will receive. In a study of applicants for an assistant professor, tenure line position (Perlman, Marxen, McFadden, & McCann, in press) 57% of the applicants failed to submit a statement on scholarship in response to a specific request for one in the job announcement.

A well-written statement on research begins with a brief history of the questions and hypotheses under investigation and then moves to current research. The current work should be described in some detail, including a sequence of studies planned for the months and years ahead. Such a statement should describe what types of students can be involved in the research (e.g., undergraduates), and the writing should be sufficiently general that someone outside this subdisciplinary area is able to understand what is written.

Applicants also should demonstrate the practical abilities necessary to maintain their own scholarship. For example, a major university research laboratory may have technicians to calibrate instruments, program and repair computers, and oversee equipment and supplies, while at your institution new colleagues may be expected to run the entire laboratory themselves.

Professional Work

Reading, viewing, or listening to the candidates' professional work yields important insights into their scholarship. Recommend that everyone submit select examples of their scholarship and professional work when they initially apply and request copies of professional work from all semifinalists and finalists. Look for rigorous thinking, appropriate and/or creative methodologies, artistic achievement, facility with data analyses, an ability to place the work within a context in the discipline, and accessibility to students.

Transcripts

Transcripts indicate coursework related to scholarship. Someone whose research interests are grounded in several graduate courses probably has a good intellectual base in the literature and published research. Other desirable coursework includes methodological training.

Design a rating form for evaluating scholarship or artistic performance using your selection criteria for the position as a guide. Such a form gives recruitment committee members structure in evaluating scholarship, facilitates comparisons among candidates, and makes it much easier for the committee to make decisions. Use the teaching portfolio rating form (Table 6.2) as a guide.

PREDICTING FUTURE CANDIDATE SCHOLARSHIP IN YOUR DEPARTMENT

The following model is presented as a way of structuring the assessment of candidates' scholarship while reading their credentials or when talking with them.

Who

Scholarship is a human endeavor. With whom has the candidate studied and worked? Certain laboratories, mentors, and artists-teachers may provide intellectual and methodological roots which will serve new colleagues well as they continue their scholarship. You also want to determine with whom candidates might collaborate in your department. Questions such as the following should be asked.

- Are there faculty in your department with whom candidates may collaborate?

- Will new colleagues continue collaborative work with their mentor or with faculty at other institutions?

- Has the candidate established a network with other scholars in his or her scholarly area?

- Can undergraduate or graduate students collaborate with the candidate for dissertations, master's theses, or undergraduate research experiences?

What

A recruitment committee also wants to assess the nature of scholarship. For example:

- What questions will the candidates study in their first few years in your department?

- Is the scholarship theory-based or applied?

- Is the scholarship directly related to the subspecialty area of the candidate or is it tangential?

- Is the scholarship narrow and specialized, does it have breadth, or does it have characteristics of both? Depth is fine for doctoral or master's students, but breadth becomes more important for collaboration with undergraduates.

- Is the scholarship area splashy or more mundane? Splash is fine if based on scientific or intellectual rigor, and it may elicit a strong interest from students. But do not overlook more typical scholarship which has the potential to contribute to the discipline and provide students opportunities to learn methods of inquiry, data collection and analysis, and the dissemination of results.

Where

Laboratory research can be conducted on campus or at other laboratories. Field research, by definition, is conducted off campus, sometimes nearby and sometimes at a distant location. Where the scholarship is conducted is important. For example, undergraduate collaborative work may be difficult if new hires must leave campus during vacation periods to visit a laboratory at a different institution or go into the field to collect the majority of their data. Other issues related to where scholarship is conducted include:

- If scholarship is done off campus, how will department members feel if new hires are absent? Will they accept this model of scholarship?

- If the scholarship is to be off campus, are funds available to support requisite travel and lodging?

When

The timetable of scholarship is critical for new hires. While a series of quickly published minute studies may not impress colleagues with their depth, neither will large scale scholarly projects never completed. While six years of probation before tenure seems a long time, the time press on new hires to do scholarship is enormous. Time issues include:

- Will the new hires hit the ground running? Can they quickly set up a laboratory or studio and continue current work?

- Are there acceptable journals and conferences where the work can be submitted and presented in a timely fashion?

- If new hires must wait for laboratories to be built or remodeled or equipment to be purchased, will these steps be completed in time to allow their scholarship to proceed? We know of one case in which a laboratory was under construction, and the new hire was promised completion upon arrival. Eighteen months after he arrived, the laboratory was completed. Obviously his planned scholarship was delayed, and he was at risk for obtaining tenure.

Why

As part of assessing teaching we talked about looking for a commitment to pedagogy. You will want to do the same when assessing scholarship. For example:

- Why do candidates work in the area they do?

- Are dedication and intellectual curiosity apparent?

- Do they enjoy scholarship? Can you sense their intrinsic satisfaction in seeing an area of inquiry or creative endeavor through from beginning to end?

How Will They Fare as Scholars?

How will the candidates' scholarship fare over time? Will you contribute to their success by supplying essential ongoing support for scholarship or is yours a seduce and abandon process of recruitment? Questions such as the following must be asked and answered.

- Can the candidate meet contractual renewal and tenure requirements with this scholarship?

- Does the scholarship seem faddish and unlikely to stand the test of time?

- Is the candidate likely to obtain extramural grant money to support the scholarship?

- Are your expectations for scholarship congruent with the time and support provided?

- Can your students really participate in and help with their scholarship or will your new colleagues use separate research projects to teach methodology and independent studies, with little time left for serious inquiry?

- Does the candidate possess the personal characteristics to produce successful scholarship? Intellectual, methodological, statistical, and writing skills cannot substitute for perseverance and common sense.

Scholarship is Difficult for Many New Faculty

Independent scholarship is a learned skill and is difficult to accomplish while one is overwhelmed with teaching responsibilities. Do not assume that prior productivity, especially for new PhDs, will continue. "…patterns of productivity are solidified when one is a new faculty member—not when one is a graduate student and not later, after settling into a professional role" (Boice, 1992, p. 81). New faculty need great assistance and encouragement to succeed with their scholarship. Boice reports that many of the new faculty he studied did almost no writing during their first two to four years, although most were recruited as potentially good teachers and scholars.

CHECKLIST

_____ Recruitment planning for scholarship needs is completed.

_____ Types of desirable scholarship are identified.

_____ Relationship of scholarship to the curriculum is understood.

_____ Selection criteria for assessing scholarship are set.

_____ Sources of information on scholarship (e.g., vitae, research statement, letters of recommendation) are established.

_____ Rating forms to evaluate scholarship are prepared.

EXERCISE

The scenario

A department was recruiting for an assistant professor, tenure line position. The selection criteria included good teaching, a program of scholarship utilizing existing laboratory space and equipment, collaborative work with undergraduates, and a willingness and ability to teach a wide variety of courses. In addition, a new course in the subdisciplinary area was needed.

Several candidates met these criteria. One rated particularly high had both postdoctoral research, and strong and successful teaching experience. She was a generalist, interested in moving to the geographic area in which the recruiting department was located, and had a genuine liking for students. However, this candidate had little public domain work despite graduate school and post-doctorate experiences, and no journal articles under review.

- *How would you proceed before deciding if this candidate should become a finalist and visit campus?*

- *What concerns would you have?*

Some answers

The recruitment committee began by reexamining its selection criteria and this candidate's abilities to meet them. It decided that the criteria were valid: a good teacher, collaborative scholarship with undergraduates, a potential to be retained, and breadth in teaching were all important.

This was the strongest candidate on the teaching criterion. Scholarship was the committee's concern because despite her lengthy training, public domain work was limited. The committee reread letters of recommendation, and telephoned both the candidate's mentor and her supervisor during the postdoctoral experience. The picture painted was of a candidate who attended to each demand in turn, never hurrying. This led to superb teaching as students never felt second to her research, but it limited her scholarship. There was little sense of urgency, though she had the "potential" to do good research.

The committee was split. Some members believed this candidate's teaching and broad background made her worthy of a campus visit. Others believed that if no substantial scholarship had been completed by now, none was likely to be forthcoming. If hired, would she meet the scholarship criterion for tenure?

The question of whether scholarly outcomes would be published could not be answered. Since other candidates met both the teaching and scholarly selection criteria this candidate was returned to the semi-finalist pool. She seemed a better fit for positions with fewer expectations for scholarship.

REFERENCES AND RECOMMENDED READINGS

Arreola, R. A. (1995). *Developing a comprehensive faculty evaluation system: A handbook for college faculty and administrators on designing and operating a comprehensive faculty evaluation system.* Bolton, MA: Anker.

Boice, R. (1992). *The new faculty member: Supporting and fostering professional development.* San Francisco, CA: Jossey-Bass.

Boyer, E. L. (1990). *Scholarship reconsidered: Priorities of the professoriate.* Princeton, NJ: Carnegie Foundation for the Advancement of Teaching.

Davidson, C. I., & Ambrose, S. A. (1994). *The new professor's handbook: A guide to teaching and research in engineering and science.* Bolton, MA: Anker.

Diamond, R. M. (1995). *Preparing for promotion and tenure review: A faculty guide.* Bolton, MA: Anker.

Diamond, R. M. (1994). *Serving on promotion and tenure committees: A faculty guide.* Bolton, MA: Anker.

Gibson, G. W. (1992). *Good start: A guidebook for new faculty in liberal arts colleges.* Bolton, MA: Anker.

Perlman, B., Marxen, J. C., McFadden, S., & McCann, L. I. (in press). Applicants for a faculty position do not emphasize teaching, *Teaching of Psychology.*

Thompson, F., & Zumeta, W. (1985). Hiring decisions in organized anarchies: More evidence on entrance into the academic career. *The Review of Higher Education, 8*, 123-138.

Warch, R. (1992). *Practicing what we preach: Scholarship and the aims of a liberal arts education.* 1991-1992 President's Report. Appleton, WI: Lawrence University, pp. 3-9.

Zanna, M. P., & Darley, J. M. (Eds.). (1987). *The compleat academic: A practical guide for the beginning social scientist.* Hillsdale, NJ: Lawrence Erlbaum.

III

THE SEARCH

ORGANIZING THE
SEARCH COMMITTEE
AND GETTING STARTED

Your department chairperson approaches you to chair a recruitment committee and you agree. What items will be on your short and long-term agendas? What would you do first? What information will you need as you begin the search? Although you have not begun your duties, do you already feel behind schedule?

We now turn to the nuts and bolts of the search, specifically all of the work which can and must be done as part of setting up the search committee, describing and advertising the position, receiving applications, and identifying good candidates for consideration. The components of this process discussed in this chapter include determining if there will actually be a recruitment, forming the recruitment committee, and initial committee tasks. In the next chapter we will discuss structuring the position and setting selection criteria, developing the position description, and getting the word out—the job description and advertising.

WILL THERE BE A RECRUITMENT?

In recent years many positions are advertised as "contingent on funding" as departments await final budget decisions. Given the amount of work to be done in a recruitment, a decision to move ahead in the face of these uncertainties carries both upside and downside risks.

On the one hand, it is possible that a recruitment committee will expend great effort only to have funding withheld. On the other, it would be devastating to decline to recruit and learn later that the department lost a position either for the next academic year or permanently because it did not try to hire. The department chairperson, an interest group head, and the potential recruitment committee chairperson need to have detailed conversations with their deans or provosts to obtain as much information as possible before making a decision to recruit when faced with uncertain funding. Ambiguities in higher education are growing, not decreasing, so this scenario will probably become increasingly common.

FORMING THE RECRUITMENT COMMITTEE

Form the Recruitment Committee Immediately

One of the first steps in academic recruiting is appointing the recruitment committee. Typically it is the dean, department chairperson, or interest group head who appoints the committee, and the entire committee membership should be identified as soon as possible after your department knows it will be allowed to recruit. If a faculty member from another department will serve on your recruitment committee, have this person designated, informed, and a working member of your group as early as possible. Determine if your committee will have student members and if so, work with them so that they will be prepared to attend important meetings and do what is expected of them. Once the committee is appointed, we recommend that its chairperson get it working as soon as possible. Beginning immediately will allow more time to initiate any necessary planning, to successfully complete the start-up tasks detailed in this chapter, to arrive at any other necessary decisions prior to writing position and job descriptions and soliciting applications, and to cope with the inevitable delays at various stages of the process.

If uncertainties exist which will make it difficult to decide on final committee membership, begin with a preliminary working committee. This group can complete initial tasks pending the formation of the permanent committee. It is helpful if the same person chairs both groups.

The Committee Chairperson

Appointment of the right committee chairperson is critical to the success of a recruitment effort. Typically a dean or department chair charges the recruitment committee and selects its chair. Chairpersons attend to affirmative action requirements and are concerned about schedules, deadlines, and the quality of decisions. They need leadership and communication skills, the ability to keep others on track, and skills in conflict resolution.

For these reasons and because of the importance of recruitment, do whatever is necessary to get the right person. Do not select someone because it is his turn or because others have assertively declined. While there is a great deal of work to be started immediately, the selection of a chair cannot be made in a haphazard fashion.

Committee Membership

Individuals should only agree to be appointed to a recruitment committee if they are willing to put in the time and effort necessary for a good search. These faculty should be a diverse group. We recommend a mix of senior and junior faculty; at least one junior faculty is highly desirable. Senior faculty can provide leadership and may have recruited in the past, while junior faculty are often more sensitive to the responsibilities of new faculty.

The committee needs members expert in the subdisciplinary area being recruited, with the background to understand the quality of the candidates' doctoral programs, recognize writers of recommendations, and evaluate scholarship. But do not have all committee members from this one specialty area. For example, in a recruitment for a violinist consider a theorist for committee membership (Ross, 1981). Such perspective is important. A recruitment committee with members from only one area is not balanced and may have a distorted view of the department, and overall student and curricular needs.

Members of a search committee need good judgment, the ability to work hard, savvy, knowledge of teaching and scholarship or a willingness to learn, integrity, and a commitment to seeing the job through. A little luck never hurt a successful recruitment effort either.

Committee Size

One of your first concerns will be how large the committee should be. In our experience three to four members is fine; there is no reason for a committee larger than five faculty members. This number provides for expertise and diverse viewpoints while remaining small enough so the committee can remain focused on its tasks, and meetings can be held at a time when all can attend. Your major goal is to have a hard working recruitment committee that will do the job and do it well.

Special Roles for Recruitment Committee Members

A recruitment committee has some important roles to fill at one of its early meetings. These roles can overlap and one committee member, such as the chairperson, often holds more than one. There are several key roles to consider filling.

A chairperson. The chairperson must follow through on committee recommendations and make sure that position descriptions and job announcements are approved through the institutional chain of command, that job announcements appear in print, that paperwork is up-to-date and current for committee meetings, and that the committee stays on task.

An ethical leader. This person will become familiar with the ethics of recruitment and will remain sensitive to, guide, and advise the committee on ethical issues throughout its work.

A teaching leader. The teaching leader serves as a source of expertise on good teaching and the use of teaching portfolios. The teaching leader serves a second function, perhaps even more important, which is to keep the spotlight on teaching throughout the recruitment. It is all too easy for a recruitment effort to begin by valuing teaching only to become enamored with candidates with high scholarly and/or grant activity, thus losing sight of earlier planning and other criteria.

A scholarship/artistic performance leader. This individual will assist the committee in attending to relevant scholarship and artistic performance abilities and potential. He or she will focus on the fit between candidates' scholarly and artistic performance interests and position needs and is sensitive to differences between quality and quantity of candidates' scholarship. This person may have some good-natured debates with the teaching leader, interchanges which will assist the committee in selecting good candidates who meet all of the selection criteria.

A recorder. The person assigned to this role will take and file meeting minutes. Typically a department or college secretary will provide support for typing correspondence and opening and filing of candidate materials. However, it is unusual for this secretary to attend committee meetings during deliberations and decision-making. It is therefore important that a faculty member on the committee be named its recorder. His tasks are relatively easy to do as the committee works, but extremely difficult to accomplish by retroactively reconstructing what took place. His minutes can detail an agenda, decisions made, utilization of selection criteria, and why known protected group and affirmative action candidates were or were not advanced to the next level of consideration. Keep the minutes brief but explanatory.

An affirmative action leader. The affirmative action leader keeps in touch with your institution's affirmative action officer throughout the recruitment. This person is knowledgeable regarding affirmative action rules and issues, and oftentimes is the same person who is the ethical leader. Sometimes the chair serves in both roles.

Other roles. These might include someone who is familiar with legal issues in recruiting (e.g., immigration, sunshine laws). Depending on the nature of the position to be filled, it may also make sense for the committee to have a resident expert on the department's or institution's laboratories, studios, or art or computer facilities.

INITIAL TASKS FOR THE RECRUITMENT COMMITTEE

A working rule is: Get started as soon as possible. Recruitment always seems to take longer than recruiting faculty hope it will, usually four months or more. It only seems like forever. There are a number of tasks the committee should do immediately. Some of these will be easily accomplished; others may take more time. Table 8.1 summarizes these initial tasks for the search committee.

TABLE 8.1

INITIAL TASKS FOR THE SEARCH COMMITTEE

- Clarify the Role and Duties of the Committee
- Agree on Committee Rules
- Agree on Committee Roles
- Find and Agree on Committee Meeting Times
- Learn About Agreements Regarding the Position
- Prepare For Departmental Planning
- Determine Budgetary Support
- Identify A Recruitment Secretary
- Read Institutional Materials
- Determine Institutional Procedures and Paperwork
- Review Policies On Hiring Spouses
- Determine if You Can Reopen An Unsuccessful Search
- Investigate Affirmative Action Requirements
- Prepare Letters
- Prepare a Form to Keep Track of Candidate Credentials
- Design Recruitment Data Bases
- Prepare for Committee Recorder Responsibilities
- Decide on Use of Electronic Mail
- Decide on How Files Will Be Circulated
- Lay Out a Time Line
- Learn About the Campus Visit Process
- Prepare Campus Visit Information
- Decide on Need for Interview Training
- Review Mentoring Process
- Maintain Communication With Departmental Faculty

Clarify the Role and Duties of the Committee

Clarify before doing. Before it begins, the recruitment committee needs
to know what it is expected to do, what fiscal support it has, and what rules
the committee will follow in doing its business. Search committees fill different roles depending on their institutions' fiscal situations, personnel rules,
and administrators' styles and views of a search. Will your search committee
only search for candidates; search and screen; search, screen, and interview;
advise the department or dean; and/or select as the final decision-maker?
Some search committees have great recommendatory power, others are less
influential.

Agree on Committee Rules

Will the committee be so formal that it follows Roberts or Sturgis rules
of order? More importantly, what will the working rules be? What is a quo-
rum? Will you allow absentee ballots? How will the committee deal with a
member who misses an excessive number of meetings or does not pay sufficient attention to candidate files? The chairperson helps set the agenda for
how the committee functions. An important maxim is: If you have a concern, we want to hear about it now. Only if the committee follows this rule
can concerns be raised and resolved in a timely fashion with everyone feeling
free to speak up. You do not want to be in a situation where concerns about
committee actions are first raised a week or a month after they occur.

Agree on Committee Roles

Committee members need to discuss and agree on who will be the ethical
and teaching leaders, as well as other roles the committee wishes to identify.

Agree on Committee Meeting Times

Typically recruitment committees need two types of meeting times. The
shorter, one-hour meeting allows for start-up responsibilities and occasionally
the discussion of candidate credentials. However, the committee will need to
agree on a second, longer meeting time for extensive discussions of candidates and serious decision making.

Learn About Agreements Regarding the Position

At the first meeting of the recruitment committee, we suggest that the
department chair, the dean, or committee chair report specifically on agreements concerning the position. In many situations the department chair has
to make a specific case in order to get the position assigned to the department, and the committee (and department) need to know the details or any
promises or agreements before you begin the planning and search. For

example, is there a top salary set with no room to negotiate above this? Must this person teach certain courses? May there be a reduction in the teaching load to do scholarship or vice versa the first year, opportunities for summer school employment, and the availability of start-up funds and moving expenses? The department needs to know about these agreements as early as possible, and not first learn about them at the time a hiring decision is being made, or later.

Prepare for Departmental Planning

The committee must decide on the need for and type of departmental planning. If you recommend departmental planning, be sure it begins early enough so that its outcomes can be incorporated in the recruitment process.

Determine Budgetary Support

The committee must clarify budgetary support. Who pays for secretarial support; postage; publishing and posting job ads; use of telephones; travel, lodging and meals if you are recruiting at professional meetings off campus; candidates' campus visits including travel, housing, and meals? You may discover there are few supports, but many expectations.

Identify a Recruitment Secretary

The committee must have secretarial help. Talk with the secretary who will be handling correspondence and letters so that this person knows how much work will be expected and when. Invite this person to your early organizational meetings so the secretary's input and practical advice are included in the process.

Read Institutional Materials

Read your institution's handbook, brochure, or pamphlet on recruitment if it has one. Such materials may be available from the provost, dean's, academic affairs' or affirmative action offices, or from your institution's office of human resources or personnel. These materials can provide information which will be extremely helpful to your recruitment. It is much better to know the rules, policies, and procedures before you do something rather than after. For example, find out how long you must store applicants' files and other recruitment process information.

Determine Institutional Procedures and Paperwork

Learn what forms and paperwork must be completed at each stage of the recruitment. Obtain these materials and make notes on who receives each piece of paperwork and at what point in your search. Talk with your dean and someone in personnel about initial contracts. Offering a candidate a two-year initial contract may help in recruitment, provides some job security, and saves on time and effort once someone is hired.

Review Policies on Hiring Spouses

Since a candidate who has a spouse also seeking employment may make a campus visit and be offered a position, now is the time for the recruitment committee to find out what institutional policies exist regarding hiring spouses. What if the spouse is bringing grant monies? Determine who will assist the spouse with finding employment, the chairperson of the recruitment or department, or someone else in the institution.

Determine if You Can Reopen an Unsuccessful Search

It is unpleasant to contemplate the failure of a search. But this possibility should be considered at the beginning of the process, and decisions should be made regarding what might be done before you find yourself choosing between hiring a marginally acceptable candidate or seeking approval to reopen the search next year.

If administrators are consulted about this question early, they may be able to provide some useful, practical information to guide your decision process. If they anticipate that budgetary stringency may cause a sweep up of vacant positions during the next academic year, you may be motivated to work even harder to unearth a good candidate from among your applicants, or you may decide to broaden your position description to expand the candidate pool. It would be wise to prepare a definition of a failed search in advance of such a meeting and a realistic estimate of its probability. Administrators will not want to sign a blank check for future recruiting costs without a good rationale. If the position can be rolled over into the next year without difficulty, reopening the search may be more attractive than the unhappy consequences of hiring a poor fit for the position.

Investigate Affirmative Action Requirements

As you prepare to begin the hiring process, you should investigate the practical requirements of equal opportunity and affirmative action hiring. It is much better to understand any requirements at the beginning of the process rather than to have deficiencies pointed out near the end. Oftentimes there are written materials which provide information and guidance for recruitment. Have the committee's affirmative action leader obtain copies and summarize the important points for the committee. Then have your institution's affirmative action officer meet with the recruitment committee or have the chairperson or affirmative action leader talk with this person. You will probably be told how your department's gender and racial composition compares with other academic units in your institution and with national availability in the discipline. If your current department faculty has fewer individuals in these categories than availability would lead one to expect, you will be encouraged to try even harder than usual to find someone from an appropriate group during the hiring process. A practical question you might ask would be, "what would happen if a Caucasian male is your most qualified candidate?"

When you talk to the affirmative action officer be sure to learn the details of your institution's affirmative action plan. You may discover that there are incentives, extra monies, and other resources available to be used to help your department meet affirmative action goals.

Your candidates do not have to make their nationality, gender, and ethnicity known in an application, but you will get this information for many of them. Talk to your affirmative action officer about your plan to have the committee recorder keep especially close track of such candidates, including a detailed record of the reasons known minority candidates are dropped from consideration at any stage of the process. This will document your fair search. Such records provide you with information that can be quite helpful in explaining why a minority candidate is not your finalist for the position, and such a record will make it clear that you dealt carefully and fairly with such applications, and worked hard to make certain that no qualified person was excluded from consideration.

While talking with the affirmative action officer, you may wish to ask about applicable immigration laws, and what visa status a noncitizen must have or be eligible to be employed.

Hiring a Good Teacher

Determine if the amount and type of TA training or professional work as a teacher you plan to require are valid criteria for the position. For example, we know of one instance where a recruitment committee had to justify one candidate with three years of tenure line university teaching over a second candidate just receiving a PhD. The issue of teaching experience as a criterion in hiring had to be understood and approved by the university's affirmative action officer.

Make sure that the teaching responsibilities do not inadvertently exclude a protected candidate. The committee must be flexible; you do not want to lose good candidates who meet nearly all selection criteria. For example, if a superb candidate cannot do lab teaching because of wheelchair inaccessibility, would your institution remodel the rooms so that access could be gained? Talking with campus experts on disability law and administrators responsible for budgetary decisions should provide the information you need regarding the possibility of purchasing needed equipment or modifying physical facilities. Current laws require reasonable accommodation to be made in such cases. If such teaching is a secondary selection criterion, you might be able to restructure the position so another course could be substituted and/or someone else teach the laboratory portion of the class.

Prepare Letters

Prepare the various form letters or e-mail messages for standard communications with applicants. These include the following:

- Acknowledgement of receipt of credentials with accompanying information (see Chapter 9)

- Acknowledgement of receipt of letters of recommendation

- Request for additional or missing information

- Inform candidates that they cannot be considered because materials arrived after the application deadline

- Inform candidates they did not meet position criteria

- Inform candidates that they have been moved to the next level of the recruitment process (optional)

- Request for semi-finalists' complete teaching portfolio

- Inform candidates that they are no longer being considered for the position as semi-finalists or finalists

- Inform candidates who are finalists but not selected for a campus interview yet

- Detail campus interview schedule for candidate with upcoming visit

- Thank you for campus visit

- Finalist rejection

These letters should be sent in a timely fashion. They should be written in a warm and gracious style, thanking candidates for their interest and effort, and wishing them every success in the completion of their PhD, their job search, and their academic career. Information in the letters should briefly but accurately communicate reasons for the candidates' status (e.g., candidates with more experience and/or better fit for the position were selected).

Prepare a Form to Keep Track of Candidate Credentials

Now is a good time to prepare the form to be inserted in each candidate's file to keep track of what materials have been received. Typically this form is a list of required or requested credentials with check marks or dates entered when the information is part of the file. Include such items as cover letter, vitae, teaching statement, research statement, letters of recommendation, transcripts, teaching portfolio, or a videotape of teaching or artistic performances.

Design Recruitment Databases

If you will have an applicant database, how will it look? Oftentimes such a database is alphabetized by the candidates' last names and includes address (including e-mail), telephone numbers, required file information (complete or what is missing), and status (e.g., did not meet position criteria, a semi-finalist). Make sure the committee chairperson or the secretary can manage this task.

Prepare for Committee Recorder Responsibilities

In order to demonstrate a good faith effort in recruitment, the committee recorder will have to keep track of a wealth of information as the search proceeds. The committee and recorder should be prepared to have the following data on file at the conclusion of the search.

- A copy of the position description
- A copy of the job description and a list of where it was posted
- Records of nominations solicited from colleagues and professional organizations
- Examples of all letters used in the search
- Records of all communications with candidates
- Records of any effort to enlarge the pool of candidates
- Candidates' folders with evaluation forms
- The core questions asked of all candidates
- A summary of decisions leading to a pool of finalists and invitations for campus visits (see below)
- Demographic descriptions of all committee members (e.g., gender, race, rank)
- Minutes from all committee meetings

Decide on Use of Electronic Mail

The committee needs to decide if it will use e-mail as a form of communication. If so, establish an e-mail address to be used by applicants seeking and sending information. Be certain to check with candidates regarding such communication if confidentiality is a concern.

Decide How Files will be Circulated

Files must be available for committee members to be read any time they want access to them, but at the same time be secure when not being read. The committee may need to have an assigned room and file cabinet keys made so that the files are accessible to its members. A signout sheet listing committee member name, date, and time materials are taken and returned is helpful so anyone seeking files knows who has them. In some searches and institutions, files must remain in the room where they are stored.

Lay Out a Timeline

Regardless of how early a search is begun, there is a limited amount of time to complete it. Recruitment during the summer is difficult, if not impossible, because of the academic year scheduling for faculty. We recommend that the search committee develop a timeline for its recruitment process. A good way to do this is to work backward in time. First identify the date by which you want an offer tendered and then move backwards to the present, identifying what has to transpire by what date to meet this goal. For example, if you want the first offer to a candidate made by April 20th, when must you hold campus visits, establish finalists, establish a pool of semi-finalists, complete initial screening, begin reading dossiers, close applications (if necessary), and publish job descriptions?

A model timeline might look like Table 8.2.

TABLE 8.2

TIMELINE FOR A SEARCH

Spring	• Department planning completed (in anticipation of a search)
September 7	• Approval to hire
	• Search committee chair appointed, committee formed and meetings begin
	• Committee roles assigned
September 21	• Position and search criteria defined
	• Position description and job announcement written
	• Job announcement submitted
November	• Job announcement published
	• Initial committee tasks defined and completed
	• Work underway to establish good candidate pool
December	• Job announcement published for a second time
January 10	• Deadline for applications—screening begins
January 21	• Applicants who do not meet position requirements identified and informed
	• Letters of recommendation and materials to complete the application requested
February 10	• Pool of semi-finalists established
	• Additional materials requested
March 1	• Teaching videotapes and portfolios, scholarly work received and reviewed
	• Telephone calls completed
	• Finalists established, campus visitors selected and invited
	• Materials sent to candidate
March 10	• Itinerary established
	• Preparations for campus visits completed
March 24	• Campus visits completed
	• **Offer to candidate made**
April 8	• Offer to another candidate made if needed
April 8 or 22	• Decisions on more campus visits, search reopened, or search closed are made
	• Paperwork completed
	• Preparations underway for arrival of new colleague

Learn About the Campus Visit Process

Now is a good time to learn if you will be allowed to bring more than one candidate to campus. If budgetary constraints exist, administrators may encourage you to invite your best candidate and then decide whether to offer that person the position, only allowing a second visitor if the first is unacceptable. We recommend bringing in at least two candidates prior to a final hiring decision (see Chapter 11).

Prepare Campus Visit Information

Prepare packets of information for candidate visits. Chapter 12 provides a listing of what might be included. By starting on this task now, the recruitment committee will have one less detail to manage as campus visits approach.

Decide on Need for Interview Training

Some recruitment committees meet with an affirmative action officer or a campus expert on interviewing to improve members' skills in interviewing in general, and selection in particular. Decide if such training would be helpful.

Review Mentoring Process

Review your mentoring process and prepare to mentor your new colleague (see Chapter 14). As Boice (1992) has noted, the success of new faculty members depends in part on the support and mentoring they receive. It makes no sense to go through all of the efforts of a recruitment and then have it be unsuccessful because the candidate hired is placed in an academic desert. Begin to worry about retention issues early; a thorough evaluation and any necessary revisions of your mentoring process may take some time.

Maintain Communication With Departmental Faculty

After the preparatory work is done, you may want to present what you have learned during a departmental meeting. Written memos to colleagues may serve the same purpose. This is a good time to inform colleagues that new hires may receive equipment and other support which are part of start-up funds not available for other purposes. If salary compression is a problem and established faculty are concerned or angry about high salaries and good support for incoming faculty, you will have time to work through such feelings so they do not interfere with the recruitment.

CHECKLIST

_____ Recruitment is approved.

_____ Balanced (viewpoints, expertise, etc.) recruitment committee is appointed.

_____ Special roles on the committee are filled.

_____ Initial committee tasks are reviewed and planned.

_____ Work is underway.

EXERCISE

The scenario

The dean informs your department in mid-March that she believes there are funds to fill the position you have been seeking for the past several years. It is not yet clear that there are sufficient funds for a tenure line position, but there are resources to support someone at the doctoral level. The dean would like the funds encumbered immediately or they may be lost, and asks that your department begin a search at once.

- *What will you need to know in order to reach a decision about whether or not to conduct a search?*

- *What would you advise the department to do?*

- *What considerations underlie your recommendations?*

- *Would you move ahead with the search?*

Some answers

While the major recruitment themes and processes have been presented as somewhat discrete issues in this book, chapter by chapter, this presentation reflects organizational necessity. In the real world of a recruitment, all the issues and problems are confluent. As in the scenario above, there is often a great deal to consider in a limited amount of time.

Many faculty members' initial response is to grab the money and run; to start the search. They know that opportunities such as this do not arise often, and that the position could be lost for years to come if the department does not act quickly. But haste is a major factor in many unsuccessful recruitment efforts. What is needed is not a hurried attempt to find candidates but a thoughtful consideration of whether there should be a search at all. The department and committee must consider questions such as the following:

- Does the department have a cadré of faculty willing to serve on a recruitment which will obviously require an immense effort in a limited amount of time? Without this commitment, it will be difficult to move forward.

- Can the dean determine if after one year the position will be made tenure line, and if so will affirmative action rules require another search?

- Does the department want to go through a major effort for a one-year appointment?

- Can the department recruit quickly enough that someone already working in a college setting could ethically accept the position if it is not offered until May or June?

- Can affirmative action considerations be defined and dealt with in such a brief time?

- Can the university approve position and job descriptions quickly, or will the recruitment committee encounter organizational delays and roadblocks as it tries to meet an early deadline?

- While the department has been lobbying for the position for several years, is the position well enough defined that recruitment can move ahead both quickly and effectively?

- Does the department know how many applicants it can expect, and is there time to do a search and screen if many candidates will apply?

- Is there a major disciplinary national meeting in the next few weeks at which the department can recruit?

- Will the dean provide funds for interviewing at conventions?

In brief, there is a serious question about whether there can be an effective and ethical recruitment based on what the dean tells the department, and on the department's degree of preparation and commitment. Without a strong recruitment committee chair and membership, and realistic financial support, we recommend the department strongly consider postponing the search until the next academic year with a list of good reasons why the opportunity for an immediate recruitment must be bypassed. Some opportunities, after careful consideration, are best left unaccepted.

REFERENCES AND RECOMMENDED READINGS

Boice, R. (1992). *The new faculty member: Supporting and fostering professional development.* San Francisco, CA: Jossey-Bass.

Marchese, T. J., & Lawrence, J. F. (1988). *The search committee handbook: A guide to recruiting administrators.* Washington, DC: American Association for Higher Education.

Ross, R. D. (1981, May). The fine art of faculty recruitment. *Music Educators Journal, 67,* 49-51.

Sommerfeld, R., & Nagely, D. (1974). Seek and ye shall find: The organization and conduct of a search committee. *Journal of Higher Education, 45,* 239-252.

Waggaman, J. S. (1983). *Faculty recruitment, retention and fair employment: Obligations and opportunities.* ASHE-ERIC Higher Education Research Report No. 2, Washington, DC: Association for the Study of Higher Education.

DEVELOPING A POOL
OF CANDIDATES

What is the most essential experience, ability, or characteristic that the successful candidate for your position must have? What is the second most important, and the third? How will you arrive at answers to these questions to make sure you hire a person who meets these requirements?

With the preliminary work outlined in Chapter 8 underway, the recruitment committee should focus its efforts on the essential first steps necessary to develop a strong pool of applicants. The specific nature and structure of the position must be decided upon, and appropriate selection criteria identified. Then a detailed position description must be developed, and finally the search committee must get the word out—the job announcement must be disseminated. Bear in mind that you will not hire someone who does not apply. The pool is critical to a good recruitment! Do whatever you can to ensure that all qualified potential candidates have an opportunity to apply.

STRUCTURING THE POSITION

Any planning you have done will facilitate the process of determining the essential nature or structure of your position, and some preliminary or near final answers should be available. Your review of the culture of the department and institution will also inform this process. Chapter 3 (Planning) and Chapters 4 (The Unique Nature of Your Position) and 5 (Recognizing Good Teaching) are preparation for the critical step of structuring your position. Once you identify and agree on the essential components of your position, you can then use these characteristics as criteria for the selection process. You must then obtain information directly related to the criteria from candidates and references. A working rule for a recruitment committee is: Get good, relevant information. This is easier said than done.

Tenure Line or Not

Whether or not you are recruiting for a tenure line position influences the nature of the opening. Non-tenure line positions filled by instructors or teaching academic staff are becoming increasingly common. If this is your situation, learn if such positions must be reevaluated each year or whether you can hire someone with a multiple-year contract. Is this contract of fixed length or will it have a rolling horizon? Will it be easily renewable if fixed length? Can it be converted to a tenure line position in the future, and will another search be required if it is?

The Specialization You Want

The nature of your department, its curriculum, and your vision of the future direction you wish to take will all contribute to the decision regarding the particular subdisciplinary specialization needed to complement your current staff. In smaller departments, it may be wise to consider seeking someone with breadth, i.e., knowledge in more than one area, and a person who can teach the variety of courses which must be covered may be difficult to find in this era of increasing academic specialization. People such as the one-person psychology department the authors met at a recent conference are a vanishing breed, but the need for such utility infielders still exists in departments and at liberal arts colleges, where they can be invaluable.

Courses and Teaching Load

What courses will the new faculty be teaching, and what will be the effective teaching load? Chapter 4 details the issues which must be considered in answering this deceptively simple question. For example, teaching the same course five times in one year is much different than teaching it once a year for five years (Sommerfeld & Nagely, 1974). Potential candidates will be particularly interested in your answers to their questions on teaching and overall work load, and these answers may determine whether the best potential candidates decide to apply.

Number of classes. The number and nature of classes to be taught must be considered. For example, a realistic class or studio schedule will facilitate good teaching, and success in carrying out other workload assignments and expectations. It will also help attract good applicants.

Primary load. If a particular specialization is being sought, what classes will be assigned in this area?

Secondary load. Develop a flexible list of additional classes from which new persons might choose to complete their teaching assignment, in order to help achieve the best fit between candidate and position. Do not let your list of additional classes end up as a selection of the least popular or most difficult courses in your curriculum, however tempting that might be.

Effective Work Load

The effective work load includes not only teaching but also artistic performance or scholarship expectations, service activities such as committee membership, and any administrative duties associated with the position. As you structure the position, you must consider its entire range of duties and try to ensure that it is realistic to expect one person to accomplish all of these. Part of this decision-making must be an honest assessment of the importance of teaching as compared to scholarship or other responsibilities.

It may be helpful to consider phasing in the new hire. If it is possible to assign a reduced scholarly load for the first semester or year, and/or to minimize initial service expectations, the development of classes and teaching skills may be greatly enhanced. Another option is to arrange a lesser teaching load for the first semester or year to ease the transition from graduate school or a previous position and facilitate the new hire's start-up.

Degrees and Experience

What degrees and experience will you require or prefer? What are the minimal qualifications for the job? The nature and level of the courses you require, program certification requirements, and a host of other variables will determine the credentials the successful candidate must possess.

There are also circumstances where professional experience is a requirement in addition to, or as an alternative for, an advanced degree. In these cases, be very clear in defining such experience so that both candidates and committee members can easily make decisions about whether particular experiences qualify the candidate for the position. The nature of the credentials sought must be carefully considered, and appropriate decisions reached, early in the recruiting process. You do not want to have to make such decisions when you are trying to choose the most acceptable candidate at the conclusion of the recruitment. That choice is difficult enough without combining it with a debate about what types of preparation and experience are really essential for success in the position.

Hiring With Advanced Rank and/or Tenure

If the nature of your position requires a person with considerable experience, you may decide to hire at the rank of Associate Professor or Professor, possibly with tenure granted on appointment. Typically these positions occupy endowed chairs or involve program leadership. These are choices that require considerable discussion, both within the department and with appropriate administrators. Hiring a faculty member with tenure is a major decision, especially in a smaller department. You need to make decisions about hiring with tenure before you advertise the position so you can word the job announcement appropriately and attract the best available candidates.

Salary

While some position salaries are listed as "open," there is always a salary limit (Sommerfeld & Nagely, 1974). To better define an appropriate salary, read job announcements and talk with recruiting faculty in departments similar to yours which are hiring for similar positions. You are then prepared for discussions with a department chair or dean who will approve a specific salary range, or allow a statement such as "the salary is in the upper range for this type of position." In brief, tell candidates what you can afford.

Whoever sets salary, often a dean or provost, must be sensitive to the problem of salary compression. Bringing in new faculty at a high salary may facilitate recruitment but lower the morale of existing faculty with lower salaries. If a salary compression problem is anticipated, the department should discuss and come to terms with it before it hires in order to minimize any resentment which might be directed toward a new colleague.

The Pool of Candidates

The pool of candidates is everything. Once the position is structured, it is wise for the recruitment committee to discuss the anticipated pool of candidates. Is the position likely to attract a few applicants or many? What is the likely mix of new and experienced candidates, those with PhDs from flagship or other institutions, and people working or not working in academia? Is this anticipated pool of applicants acceptable to the committee? If not, you need to restructure the position. If so, determine your selection criteria.

SET YOUR SELECTION CRITERIA

You should now be ready to identify the selection criteria for your position. This should be a relatively brief list, in priority order, of the most important position characteristics. Each candidate's characteristics and experiences will be evaluated using these criteria.

There is another advantage to the use of overtly defined selection criteria. "Improvisation invites conflict" (Marchese & Lawrence, 1988, p. 4), and selection criteria provide an organized structure for decision making.

Avoid Self-Defeating Selection Criteria

You do not want to have experiences or credentials so high or specific that good people do not bother to apply. You want the strongest possible pool of candidates from which to make your choice.

In a recruitment in the authors' department, the prioritized selection criteria read as follows:

- PhD Developmental Psychologist: Must be able to teach child/adolescent with secondary abilities in social psychology.

- Excellent teaching abilities and/or potential.

- Breadth in disciplinary background and specialty.

- Research program which involves collaborative work with both graduate and undergraduate students.

- Retention potential. An interest in a regional university, teaching, and/or midwest location.

What the reader should note is (1) the limited number of criteria; (2) the fact each can be measured; (3) that other criteria such as scholarly potential will certainly be used in selection but that these are not primary; and (4) that these criteria provide a focus for the recruitment committee as they read credentials and select finalists for the position. The rating form used to evaluate credentials should reflect the selection criteria.

Preparation of Rating Forms

Once selection criteria are established, the committee can begin work on the rating form it will use for initial evaluation of the entire set of credentials, and on other forms for specifically evaluating teaching portfolios (an example is provided in Chapter 6) and scholarship or artistic performance as the pool of candidates is reduced. Anyone reading your evaluation forms should be able to broadly define your selection criteria. An example of a rating form for candidate file credentials can be found in Table 9.1.

TABLE 9.1

RATING FORM FOR EVALUATING CANDIDATE CREDENTIALS

_____ Folder number   _____Candidate Name

Overall rating

1——————— 2 ——————— 3 ——————— 4 ——————— 5
highest   satisfactory   unsuited to
priority   our needs

Degree status:

Educational background (including undergraduate preparation):

Teaching

Teaching experience

Teaching interests

Teaching support needed (equipment, TAs, etc.)

Quality of teaching (letters of reference for teaching, candidate teaching statement)

Teaching fit (position needs and candidate experience and interests)

Scholarship and Artistic Performance

Research/scholarship/artistic performance experience and publications/
    presentations

Research/scholarship interests

Scholarship/performance support needed (space, equipment, etc.)

Quality of scholarship/performance (letters of reference for scholarship,
    candidate scholarship statement)

Scholarship fit: position needs and candidate experience and interests

Service

Comments

Candidates Also Have Selection Criteria

Keep in mind that your candidates will also have selection criteria. While ideally one thinks of them as seeking "...meaning, prestige, community, and time to devote to study and reflection" (Getman, 1992, p. ix), in our experience many candidates are seeking any acceptable academic job. Some may want to use entry-level positions to improve their credentials so they can get their next job in a more desired location. Nonetheless, the best-qualified candidates are in most demand, and they will carefully evaluate elements of the position such as teaching load or opportunities for scholarship.

THE POSITION DESCRIPTION

After structuring the position and developing selection criteria, the next step is the creation of a complete position description. Remember that this is not the job announcement you will publish in the relevant journals and vacancy lists, so it can be as long as is necessary to spell out all aspects of the position including expected teaching and other duties. It should be sent to job applicants along with your initial acknowledgment of their application to ensure that they clearly understand the exact nature of the available position. This knowledge will (1) help applicants decide if they are really interested in pursuing the position; (2) identify what they will be required to submit; and (3) provide the background for more informed questions throughout the recruitment process. The position description may include, but is not limited to, information such as that suggested in Table 9.2.

Hiring a Good Teaching Faculty Member

The position description communicates the priorities of the hiring department, and there are several ways you can communicate the importance of good teaching.

- State clearly and concisely that good teaching is important.

- Describe support for good teaching (e.g., teaching excellence centers, seminars on teaching, and/or mentoring).

- State initial requirement for a teaching statement and its content.

- Describe requirements for what is to be enclosed in a teaching portfolio and who will be asked to submit one.

- Describe any other teaching related information you want submitted.

TABLE 9.2

INFORMATION FOR A POSITION DESCRIPTION

- Specializations needed

- Department name

- Tenure line position or not. If not, title and length of contract (academic staff, instructor—one year, two year, etc.)

- Funding for the position is secure or hiring is contingent on funding being made available

- Rank if tenure line

- Required job qualifications (education and experience, knowledge/skills/abilities)

- Specify preferred credentials

- Description of teaching duties/assignments

- If good teaching is a prerequisite, say so

- Professional activity (scholarship, artistic performance, etc.) expected

- Service/administrative duties

- Availability of faculty development funds, internal scholarship grants, or teaching excellence center support

- Period of employment, 9 months or full year

- Date position is available

- Date screening of applications will begin

- Date application period closes

- Salary range

- Description of department (number of faculty, number of majors,

- degrees granted, and other relevant information)

- Description of university/college

- Description of the geographic area including quality of life, cost of living, etc.

- Curriculum vitae needed

- Number of letters of recommendation needed or number of names to be submitted (committee will contact)

- Teaching and/or scholarship statement needed

- If teaching portfolio required of semi-finalists, say so

- If videotapes of teaching are required of semi-finalists, say so

- If audiotapes and videotapes of representative music performances or slides of artistic works are required of semi-finalists, say so

- Transcripts needed, if any, when making initial application, and if required, official or unofficial

- Studio, laboratory, or research space

- A brief description of the interview process or in music, the audition process

- State whether information about candidates must be revealed upon request (sunshine laws)

- The person to contact if more information is desired (name, address, phone, e-mail address)

Getting the Word Out:
The Job Announcement and Other Considerations

Now you must convert your position description into job announcements (ads) and other means of calling attention to your vacancy. The formal position description provides the basis for the development of the briefer job description for advertising and posting.

The Job Announcement

Reading job announcements in your placement publications and relevant journals will provide many examples of specific language and content you may want to consider. It will also reveal that some announcements are sterile, uninteresting, or unclear, and a few are all of the above. Your job description should be clear and well written.

Since the job announcement is briefer than the position description, decisions must be made about what to include and what to omit. Typically the job announcement contains the information needed to adequately describe the position and the application process. For example, a job announcement would:

- Identify the disciplinary specialization sought.

- Tell what types of candidates will be preferred (preferences should reflect selection criteria).

- Indicate the type of position (e.g., tenure line or not, title of position—assistant professor, instructor).

- Identify your institution and department.

- State if funding is secure or anticipated.

- State excellent teaching is an important criterion for the candidate selected, assuming it is.

- Request a curriculum vitae.

- State if teaching and/or research statements are required.

- State if copies of scholarship should be submitted (recent, select, or all).

- State if audio and/or videotapes of musical teaching or performance, or slides of artistic work are required.

- Provide procedures for submission of letters of recommendation.

- Ask for official, unofficial, or no transcripts at this time. We recommend unofficial ones. Finalists can be asked to obtain official transcripts.

- State when screening begins and the closing date for applications.

- State if pre-screening is to occur at professional meetings and list the meetings.

- Contain a line or two about the assets (e.g., beauty, climate, culture) of the area.

One word of advice. If you are not certain you will obtain a reasonable number of applicants who meet all requirements of the position, redefine the most uncertain of these requirements as preferable. That way your larger pool will meet the posted requirements, and you may avoid having to reopen the search because you trapped yourself with what turned out to be overly restrictive job requirements.

Questions Prior to Posting Job Announcements

Prior to advertising, there are a number of questions you will need to have answered:

- Who must approve your job description and ad before it can be posted?

- Does your dean or college require the inclusion of any specific information (e.g., writing of grants, scholarship)?

- What affirmative action language, if any, must be included?

- Where do you want to advertise?

- Are you required to advertise in any specific publication(s)?

- Who pays for the ads—the department, the college? A detailed and lengthy job announcement means increased publication costs. Talk with your department chairperson or dean about your advertising budget.

- Will you use only print advertisements?

- Will you use convention placement bureaus?

- Will you place ads on e-mail bulletin boards?

- Will you mail job announcements to relevant doctoral-granting departments, colleges, or universities?

- Would it be helpful to place phone calls to faculty at doctoral-granting or other institutions?

The goal of publishing and posting job announcements is to develop a strong pool of applicants from which to select finalists. The committee may find that past advertising, while extensive, included some announcements that did not really contribute to the quality or number of applicants. If you advertise in places consulted by all good candidates, other ads may just duplicate your effort and waste money. Conversely, the committee may decide a stronger pool of applicants will result with more extensive dissemination of the job announcement.

We recommend having your job announcements published at least twice in the most widely read journals or job bulletins for faculty openings in your discipline. Publishing them more than once allows wording to be corrected if errors occur, and puts them before potential candidates for a longer period of time.

Recruiting at Professional Meetings

Some searches use the placement bureaus at conventions or professional meetings both to post position announcements and to conduct initial interviews. These searches combine reaching candidates with an initial screening to establish semi-finalists. This process is sometimes used because of the tradition of recruiting in a discipline (e.g., business accounting) or the need to fill a position late in the academic year. On other occasions there may be a real need for initial screening. We are aware of recruitments where well over 500 candidates applied for a single position. In these cases, the recruitment committee chairperson and/or committee members may decide to attend one or more professional meetings to screen candidates so a semi-finalist pool can be more easily developed.

In such cases it is even more important that the committee has developed clear and prioritized selection criteria. Those recruiting at the meeting should talk beforehand about what they will be looking for, and they should complete a rating form for each applicant with whom they meet. While meeting with and evaluating candidates at a professional meeting can be an efficient use of time, beware of fatigue, both for you and the candidates with whom you are meeting. As a day of interviewing progresses, everyone's productivity begins to fall. You may want to schedule breaks for the interviewing faculty members, or not schedule them for a complete day. Assess the fatigue of candidates carefully. If near the end of a day a candidate looks especially fatigued, suggest rescheduling if possible.

Letters of Recommendation

The job announcement tells candidates how many letters of recommendation you want and whether you want them sent directly or prefer names of references to contact. We recommend:

• Asking for names to contact. This format allows you to ask for specific information reflecting your selection criteria; e.g., candidates' teaching ability, statements on their collegiality, or about their scholarship potential.

- A minimum of three letters and no more than five.

- Letters on file (e.g., placement bureaus) be accepted only when necessary, such as for candidates overseas.

Setting Deadlines

Legal and/or affirmative action considerations may require you to set a closing date for applications. Make certain you decide what will constitute an application at that point, so partial files may be completed as necessary or rejected as arriving too late for consideration.

The recruitment committee must set a date to begin considering applications. We recommend about four weeks after job announcements appear in your major publications. Setting a date too far in the future wastes time. If you set the date too early, committee members are constantly reading new applications and mixing them with old ones on which decisions may have already been made. Expect applications to arrive up to and on the day of your stated deadline and after. Typically you cannot consider applications submitted late; determine your institutional policy on this matter.

CHECKLIST

_____ Position is structured.

_____ Selection criteria are set.

_____ A rating form is developed reflecting selection criteria.

_____ Position description is written.

_____ Decisions are made on issues such as letters of recommendation and deadlines.

_____ Job announcement is prepared.

_____ Search process (print advertising, posting, and initial interviews at professional meetings, etc.) is developed.

EXERCISE

The scenario

A department of 30 has had several retirements and has received permission to recruit three tenure line faculty. The teaching load is four courses/semester (eight total) while nationally the average load is four to six a year. Additionally, some faculty have as many as four different course preparations for at least one of their two semesters. In some departments in the university, faculty can "buy-down" from eight cours-es a year if they engage in ongoing scholarship. Because of the numbers of freshman courses and general education students taught, no such opportunity exits in this department.

Other aspects of the positions are mixed. Positively, the university has an internal grants program for scholarly activities, and salary for the positions is competitive. More negatively, there are insufficient funds for faculty to attend conferences, and in addition to high-quality teach-ing, standards for tenure include publication. Further, senior faculty are not good role models for scholarship.

Nonetheless, attracting applicants will not be problematic. The recruitment committee expects in excess of 500 applicants for the three positions. Because of the number of applicants, finding candidates with relatively good fit for the position should not be a problem.

- *How should one proceed with this recruitment?*

Some answers

The search committee had no difficulty in beginning its work and selec-tion criteria were clearly defined, including specialty area expertise for candi-dates. Given the number of applications, this search needed to be an effi-cient one, with candidates quickly but thoroughly screened, thus expediting establishment of a pool of semi-finalists and finalists. Close communication with departmental colleagues prepared them for the six or more campus vis-its which would take place.

The committee decided, correctly, that this is a recruitment effort in which retention should be a focus. Because of an uneven playing field between this department's teaching and work load and other positions nationally and within the university, the committee looked for candidates with maturity and experience in teaching. Candidates who had the ability or potential to cope with the high workload would be given preference. Open communication was emphasized. While not glossing over problems in the positions, positive elements were emphasized: internal grants, a good cadré of younger faculty in the department, good quality of life in the area, and a mentor program allowing as much individual attention as new faculty want.

REFERENCES AND RECOMMENDED READINGS

Boice, R. (1992). *The new faculty member: Supporting and fostering professional development.* San Francisco, CA: Jossey-Bass.

Davidson, C.I., & Ambrose, S. A. (1994). *The new professor's handbook: A guide to teaching and research in engineering and science.* Bolton, MA: Anker.

Getman, J. (1992). *In the company of scholars: The struggle for the soul of higher education.* Austin, TX: University of Texas Press.

Gibson, G. W. (1992). *Good start: A guidebook for new faculty in liberal arts colleges.* Bolton, MA: Anker.

Marchese, T. J., & Lawrence, J. F. (1988). *The search committee handbook: A guide to recruiting administrators.* Washington, DC: American Association for Higher Education.

Ross, R. D. (1981, May). The fine art of faculty recruitment. *Music Educators Journal, 67,* 49-51.

Sommerfeld, R., & Nagely, D. (1974). Seek and ye shall find: The organization and conduct of a search committee. *Journal of Higher Education, 45,* 239-252.

Waggaman, J. S. (1983). *Faculty recruitment, retention and fair employment: Obligations and opportunities.* ASHE-ERIC Higher Education Research Report No. 2, Washington, DC: Association for the Study of Higher Education.

10

SCREENING CANDIDATES AND SELECTING SEMI-FINALISTS

You have a pile of 75 applications. Now what will you do? Your applicants have a variety of strengths and weaknesses, but none of them is ideal in every respect. What will you look for as you read candidates' credentials? How will you get good information on each, and how will you use it to select the people who best fit your position?

You should now be ready to begin the process of reviewing credentials and evaluating candidates. This chapter describes the steps you must take and the decisions you must make as you move from placing job descriptions to establishing a small pool of the most qualified applicants, from which you will select your finalists and campus visitors. We start with establishing (and maintaining) good communication with candidates. This practice should continue throughout any search.

COMMUNICATION WITH CANDIDATES

What follows is written from the perspective of a committee that will be screening candidates' credentials rather than interviewing at conferences, since recruitment at professional meetings is done less frequently. All tenets of good communication apply equally to both processes.

As you begin to screen applications, you will need to communicate with candidates for many reasons: to acknowledge their application, to seek missing information, to indicate that you have decided that some are not a good fit for your position, and to conduct telephone interviews with the most promising.

Maintain Open Communication

You should strive to inform candidates openly of where they stand in your search process and to answer as best you can any questions they have. You lose nothing by being open in your communication, and you gain the trust and appreciation of your applicants.

Another outcome of continuous and open communication is the development of a positive reputation for the recruiting department among the candidates' peers and faculty. This can be advantageous when you recruit again.

Communicate Promptly

Prompt communication will alert candidates to provide needed information in time for their credentials to receive further review. Boice (1992) notes that candidates perceive long silences during recruitment as a problem. Silence after initial acknowledgement of applications generates a feeling that the campus does not care enough to keep applicants informed of their status or is not interested in them. You do not want to encourage good candidates to look elsewhere.

Candidates can best plan their lives and deal with other employment options when search committees apprise them of their standing as soon as it is known. We have heard stories about search committees that never respond or communicate after an application has been sent. This behavior can be most politely described as rude. One person once went on an academic job interview and then never received any subsequent communication informing him of his standing. Obviously he did not get the job, but he found out a lot about the department and its recruitment committee. Even no communication is communication of a sort.

The Use of Electronic Mail

Many candidates will provide an e-mail address in their vitae, and the recruitment committee should take advantage of this method of communication if it has access to e-mail. Use of this medium allows a rapid exchange of information without the need for both sides to be available simultaneously, as in telephone communication. E-mail also can save the committee time and effort. If your secretary has access and knowledge, a separate e-mail address can be created for the search committee. Your secretary can then check this mail regularly and answer simple inquiries about the status of applications without troubling committee members. You can use this means to identify times when candidates will be available for phone calls as well, saving both time and phone costs. You can easily create form letter responses within which specific questions or comments may be inserted for e-mail use.

When using e-mail be careful about confidentiality, being sure that e-mail messages are as secure as possible and available only to the candidate. We will assume that you will use normal mail for most of your letters to candidates, but encourage you to facilitate and supplement your correspondence with e-mail whenever possible.

ACKNOWLEDGING THE APPLICATION

Your first opportunity to communicate with an applicant is when you acknowledge receipt of the application, and the committee should send such acknowledgements as soon as possible. Your acknowledgement should include a variety of information such as:

- A statement that the application has been received, and an expression of appreciation for the interest shown

- Your formal position description

- Requests for teaching and research statements, or audio and visual tapes, or slides if they have been requested but not provided

- A request for the applicant's e-mail address, if you will be using this form of communication and the candidate has not already supplied it

- Information on the search process, including its timeline

In all communications, keep in mind that you are selling the position, department and institution, even with the earliest contacts with candidates. The timeliness and content of your letters communicates a variety of informal information to candidates.

INITIAL SCREENING

Initial screening is usually a process of identifying candidates who do not meet position requirements. Ranking the qualified candidates comes later. As the last chapter indicated, your job descriptions announcing the position should contain a request for some basic information from those making an initial application for the job. Typically you will ask for a curriculum vitae, statements on teaching and scholarship, and the names of references or letters of recommendations from those individuals. This is the information (including the applicant's cover letter) that you will use as you begin the review and screening of credentials.

Eliminating applicants who do not meet important job criteria is typically a relatively easy task. In each recruitment there are applicants who do not have the degrees, training, specialty expertise, or experiences which are prerequisites for the job. You need to decide if everyone on the recruitment committee will read all folders or if one or two members can do the initial screening. Unless you have over 50 or so applications we recommend that everyone on the committee read each file. Even by skimming files, recruiting faculty will pick up different relative strengths and weaknesses for candidates. A committee can go through candidates alphabetically and arrive at consensus on those to be deleted quickly and easily. Do not spend time debating the merits of individuals at this point. If they have any promise, save them for a later, closer look.

Communicate With Candidates Who are Screened Out

As applicants fail to advance through your search, remove them from your pool of active candidates and inform them immediately. Communicate this information via regular mail and be polite, thanking candidates for their application and providing general reasons why they were not selected for further consideration (specialization, degree, experiences, or others better fitted to your unique position). Inform them that you had many qualified candidates, and wish them well in their professional work and search for a position.

Why Candidates are Removed from Consideration

Your department chair, dean, or institution's affirmative action officer all may need data on the status of certain candidates throughout the search, or even after completion. Create a master list of candidates and document why candidates are no longer being considered for your position, either by using a code number or writing out the reason. These data are easy to generate as the search process unfolds but time consuming to reconstruct.

IDENTIFYING SEMI-FINALISTS

Is the Entire Pool of Sufficient Size?

After your initial screening of applications, you should pause and decide if you have a sufficient number of qualified applicants to continue the search. For example, if you only have 10 applicants, and none are women or minorities, or you have many fewer applications than expected, it may be wise to reevaluate your job announcement and where it was placed to determine if there is something you can do to expand the pool of candidates. Remember, a strong pool of the best available candidates is essential to a successful search. Any steps which expand your pool will be well worth the effort, regardless of whether there are affirmative action obligations. If the pool is of sufficient size, continue your work of selecting semi-finalists.

Obtain Letters from References

The next step is to obtain letters of recommendation if the committee is asking for writers' names and to contact them directly. Once your letter to references is prepared, your secretary can write to each indicating the candidate who has asked for a reference letter, the position for which the candidate is applying, and what information you seek. Be sure to include a deadline for the letter and a copy of your job description. E-mail can assist in sending reminders.

Letters of recommendation can be excellent sources of information about the candidate's background and ability, and recruitment committees often ask applicants to arrange to have three to five such letters sent directly to the committee. This procedure has the advantage of making the applicant responsible for contacting the references and arranging for letters to be sent, but it has the great disadvantage of leaving the letter writer to guess what it is you would like to know.

We suggest that the committee ask for the names of three to five references rather than for letters, and that these individuals be contacted with a list of the specific questions the committee has regarding candidate characteristics. Asking for letters allows you to avoid the common problem of reading statements about candidates who are described as good teachers even though the writer has never seen the candidate teach, are all fine people, and described time and again as excellent researchers/performers/artists. We are suggesting that rather than the standard letter of recommendation you want a letter of evaluation, specifically including information relevant to your selection criteria. Many applicants will automatically arrange to have the typical letters sent, but you can still follow up with the questions in which you are particularly interested. The content you may wish to request tends to fall into three broad categories.

Teaching. Be specific in what you want to know about the candidate's teaching. Does the candidate do well in large and small classes? Could she teach well at both graduate and undergraduate levels? Can she teach classes outside her specialty area?

Scholarship and artistic performance. Positively, writers of letters seem well prepared to respond regarding candidates' scholarship and artistic performance, and you can expect the responses to include some predictable content. Nonetheless, your committee may wish for additional information on scholarship and performance, including the ability to work independently, cost of essential equipment, and secondary specialties.

Collegiality and service. There are other important characteristics that contribute to success as a faculty member, and you want to be sure to obtain information on candidates' potential citizenship in your department, their abilities and interest in doing required faculty service. Do they get along well with others, and have they had experience in working on committees?

In brief, when you contact the reference, there are three specific types of questions you might ask regarding a candidate. We present sample questions to ask writers of letters of evaluation in Table 10.1. These questions are not meant to be exhaustive but rather illustrative of what references might be asked. You would not ask for all of this information; the letter of evaluation would be far too long. As with other ideas in this book, pick and choose the questions which will be most helpful in your recruitment. A selection of those questions most relevant to the requirements of your position should produce some unusually useful responses.

We recommend that references receive a brief letter or postcard from your committee acknowledging their letter, thanking them, and emphasizing how much you appreciate their time and effort in assisting your recruitment committee. These brief feedback letters engender good will and are common courtesy.

Reducing the Number of Applications Remaining

If you have a large pool of applicants whose status is still active, it is probably wise to go through the files again and remove those who are the poorest fit. We would suggest reducing the pool to no more than 50.

The pool of applicants is now smaller, but the hard work is just beginning. Now the committee has to winnow and sift through these applicants, all of whom meet the important criteria for the position. Try to ensure that the files are complete and can be read and evaluated in detail. The purpose of this work is to select a small pool of about 10 semi-finalists. You may have fewer than or slightly more than 10 applicants remaining when you have completed this task. For example, if you expect a competitive, difficult search with the possibility that several of your finalists may take positions elsewhere, leave yourself some leeway. Instead of a pool of 10 semi-finalists, with all other candidates informed that they are no longer being considered, leave the next five or 10 applicants in a "still being considered" category.

As you read the files, take nothing for granted. It is not that candidates intentionally deceive, but if information is not spelled out in detail assume you will have to get the facts. If you have questions, get answers. If you call references for further information, keep in mind that you cannot ask them questions which you are not allowed to legally ask candidates during an interview.

TABLE 10.1

TOPICS FOR LETTERS OF EVALUATION

Questions on Teaching

- Would this person be happiest in a major research university doing primarily scholarship or artistic performing?

- Does this person really want to teach?

- Has the candidate indicated an interest in working closely with students both in and out of the classroom?

- Have you had many opportunities to see this individual teach?

- What is your assessment of the candidate's teaching ability?

- What is the quality of interactions with students, and on what observations do you base this assessment?

- Will the candidate be effective teaching both large (100+ students) and small classes?

- Will this person teach well at both graduate and undergraduate levels?

- Does this person have breadth as well as depth of knowledge in the discipline, and in what content areas outside the specialty area?

- Is this person aware of the ethical dilemmas which can arise in teaching and research? For example, does this person behave responsibly with students outside the classroom, and is grading done objectively and fairly?

Questions on Research-Scholarship-Artistic Performance

- Does the candidate's research require specialized equipment and space? What are the start-up costs? Can apparatus be shared?

- Does the individual have a secondary area of research interest or expertise?

- What is the quality of the individual's output to date?

- Will she be able to continue or develop her own independent research program after leaving the mentor's lab or studio?

- Could he collaborate with other faculty?

- Will he be able to work collaboratively with undergraduates or graduate students in his scholarship?

- Will she be able to maintain research productivity with a full teaching load and various service responsibilities?

- Will he publish?

- Does the individual maintain a consistently high level of artistic performance before the public?

Questions on Service and Qualifications as an Academician

- Does this person really want a career in academia? Does he have any idea how much work it is to be an academician?

- Will he be a good department citizen?

- What is her capacity for pursing career goals while maintaining respect for confidentiality and tolerance of others' points of view?

- Will she work effectively with colleagues of many varying interests?

- Will he seek interaction with and the friendship of other faculty?

- What is his level of emotional maturity in interacting with students and colleagues?

- Will he devote as much time and energy to his department and institution as he will to relationships with others across the country and to national organizations?

- Have you ever observed this individual's performance as a member of a committee? How would you describe this performance?

- What is his most significant weakness?

- Briefly describe the candidate (e.g., thoughtful, energetic, juggles many projects at once, good sense of humor).

- Does the candidate wear well?

Leave enough time for several passes through the applications. We recommend that every member of the recruitment committee completely read every remaining file, but beware of what is called the heavy work phenomenon (Marchese & Lawrence, 1988). Reading 125 or more sets of credentials can quickly lower the proportion of each file that is really read and considered. The initial screening and deletion of the least competitive candidates will reduce the number of applicants to a manageable number fairly quickly. When you get to this point, be sure to adjust your procedures from a focus on deleting candidates to a focus on keeping good applicants in the running.

Decide on Candidate Advocates

Consider assigning committee advocates for each candidate. Advocates read candidate materials very closely and present a brief synopsis of the candidate's credentials. Advocates also can be used to present semi-finalists' credentials as you select finalists.

When in Doubt, Leave Candidates in the Running

Keep in mind that once candidates are removed from consideration and so informed, you will no longer be considering them. If you err, do so by retaining credentials for further consideration. If a committee member asks that a candidate be left in the running, do so. You have little to lose and much to gain.

Consider moving any candidate, but especially known minority or protected candidates who are on the border, up to the next level, and so note in your records. This allows full consideration for individuals who may have atypical career paths or have attended institutions not well-known to committee members, but who may have the abilities to do the teaching, scholarship, and other work you need done.

Good File Management and Record Keeping

Committee members may begin to feel as if they are experiencing a paper blizzard. If the committee and its recorder have done their job as the search unfolded, the information needed to document a good faith search effort (see Chapter 8) has been collected and is on file. Accurate record keeping facilitates knowing where submitted materials are, what is missing, and what has been reviewed. If this data collection is incomplete, obtain or prepare the missing material as soon as possible. We cannot overemphasize the importance of workable and accurate record keeping.

Sources of Information in Selecting Semi-Finalists

Cover letters. Candidates often put important information in their cover letters, and these should be read carefully and used in rating candidates.

The teaching statement. In Chapter 9 we suggested that you ask applicants for a teaching statement. This statement should help you to decide if an applicant has sufficient potential fit for the position to be advanced to the next level of consideration.

If you are using a form to evaluate candidates' credentials (see Chapter 9 for an example), use each applicant's statement as part of the basis for your rating of teaching. You must keep your selection criteria clearly in mind so that new PhDs with limited teaching but considerable teaching potential can receive ratings comparable to good experienced teachers. The committee's teaching leader will be helpful in this task.

In reading teaching statements, look for good writing skills, depth, a working knowledge of what is involved in teaching, and other criteria which may be important for your individual search (e.g., collaborative work with students outside the classroom, use of essay examinations). Chapter 5 on recognizing good teaching will be helpful in establishing specific teaching criteria.

The research-performing arts statement. The research statement and/or vitae should describe the research experience, interests, and specialization of the applicant. Relevant information includes the candidates' publications, papers, presentations, and artistic performances; type and amount of laboratory or studio space needed; and the nature and cost of essential equipment.

As with the teaching statement, committee members can rate applicants on the various indices of scholarship you have established as important criteria, including the following dimensions:

- Is the statement well written?

- Does it show intellectual depth and knowledge of the area under study?

- Is the type of scholarship or artistic work described a good fit for the position?

- Will applicants dovetail with current faculty and provide them intellectual company and synergy? Or will the candidates be somewhat isolated in their scholarly or artistic interests?

- Can your department or institution support the scholarship or work being described with space, equipment, and students?

- Is there an area of secondary interest and expertise?

- Is there an indication that the candidate can pursue an independent scholarship or artistic performance agenda in the absence of a mentor or established facilities?

If the teaching and research statements are missing or do not contain sufficient information, ask for more information when you acknowledge receipt of the application. While you may be tempted to conclude that someone who has not provided the information you want is not a promising candidate for your position, remember that many applicants will have limited experience or guidance in preparing such credentials. You do not want to miss an outstanding candidate because you did not take the time to request information that is probably readily available.

In the performing arts, audio and/or videotapes of musical performances or slides of artistic work are invaluable evidence for selecting and confirming a semi-finalist pool of candidates. Audio and videotapes may be evaluated either by individual committee members privately, or by the committee as a whole. In one search by a music department, one videotape of a candidate conducting an orchestra was described as enthralling. Neither letters of reference nor the candidate statement captured the ability and artistry of this applicant. Her videotape was critical in moving her up to the pool of semi-finalists.

Letters of recommendation/evaluation. Among the best potential sources of information regarding the training, abilities, and personality of candidates are the writers of letters of recommendation. Unfortunately, many references submit what can best be described as generic letters; sometimes they seem to have been written from the candidate's vitae by someone unacquainted with the person in question. This is why we suggest you obtain letters responding to specific questions your recruitment committee has.

If the response to any of your questions is incomplete, do not hesitate to call to get additional information. Some people will be much more willing to talk than to take the time to write a complete letter. Do not forget to take good notes on what you are told so you can provide a summary to the rest of the committee.

Ascertain the relationship of the letter writer to the candidate. A senior faculty serving as a dissertation chairperson has more credibility than a graduate-student colleague of the applicant. In assessing the content of letters of recommendation, keep track of how long the writers have known candidates and in what ways they have worked with them (e.g., observed them or supervised them in teaching or scholarship).

General Issues in Reading Files

As you read applicants' cover letters, vitae, teaching and scholarship statements, and letters of recommendation, there are a variety of other criteria which enter the decision-making arena.

Characteristics of successful faculty. Many faculty reading applicant credentials compare them to an implicit model of what it is that they believe successful faculty members are and do. It is often helpful if committee members talk about these internal models and make them explicit. If this is done, you can discuss your ratings of candidates and decisions about them with some knowledge of your colleagues' perspectives. Recruitment committees may want to ascertain candidate potential in areas such as:

Fit. You should always read credentials with an eye toward good fit. This ability to fit in goes beyond written selection criteria to whether a candidate would be happy at your type of institution or in your specific department. Look also for what candidates do not say. For example, some candidates present beautifully written cover letters and statements on scholarship, with little mention of teaching. Do they fit your idea of the type of person you want as a finalist? Be careful about making assumptions, however. Some candidates who emphasize scholarship in their credentials may do so because they believe this is what is expected from them, and may be quite happy in a position in which equal weight is given to teaching and scholarship.

Academic pedigree. Most recruitment committees want intelligent candidates with strong academic backgrounds. Doctoral degrees from well-established, highly-ranked institutions and doctoral programs are typically valued more than those from other institutions. A well-selected committee will know of strong graduate programs in unlikely institutions; do not judge the quality of candidates' educations merely on institutional name.

Other academic background questions include types of postdoctoral experiences, if any, and their nature. Is the applicant a member of honor societies? Have they received other honors?

Gaps. Is the information that candidates present congruent with their years of experience or time since degree? If there are gaps of a year or two, were the candidates engaged in productive work not mentioned or did they take time off to do other things? Be careful in such inquiries, as some activities may not be legal considerations in recruitment and hiring.

Maturity. Another candidate quality often assessed is maturity—as distinct from age. Faculty work extremely hard in multi-faceted roles. Recruitment committees want to hire a colleague who can handle these pressures and roles with some aplomb and grace. They look for candidates who will be happy and comfortable in the faculty role. Candidates' past experiences, letters of recommendation, and written teaching and scholarship statements provide insights into their maturity, yet this remains a difficult characteristic to adequately assess.

Candidates' expectations. Form an impression of what each candidate expects from the position being filled. If expectations are for a leisurely career in an ivory tower, these hopes may not fit the position you have available (or any you have heard of recently). Some candidates simply have unrealistic expectations. Sophisticated scholarship requiring expensive equipment may not be possible in a university with limited resources. A department in which teaching is regularly discussed by its faculty is rare (Boice, 1991), even in departments truly valuing pedagogy. Some candidates expect bright and intellectually alive students who do brilliantly in class and laboratories. These characteristics may not describe your students, many of whom may need a lot of faculty advice and guidance to approach their academic potential.

Explicit criteria for new faculty success also exist. Boice (1992) identifies interrelated areas in which successful new faculty excel. These include:

Involvement. Immersion in the campus community outside the classroom and department. Successful individuals are actively involved.

Regimen. Successful new faculty manage their tasks well. The real need is not time but task management, deciding what needs to be done first and how much time to devote to it.

Self-management and social networks. Professional work has a balance between scholarship and teaching on the one hand, and social networking (support from and spending time with colleagues) on the other. Successful new faculty are collegial, not isolated.

Outcome

You now have a pool of about ten semi-finalists. The next chapter describes the selection of finalists and decisions on whom to invite for campus visits.

CHECKLIST

_____ All letters and requests for information are prepared.

_____ You are prepared to run an open search with prompt communication.

_____ A decision has been made about use of e-mail, and a search committee address has been established.

_____ All materials to send candidates with your application acknowledgement are prepared.

_____ Initial screening completed (remove candidates who do not meet required criteria).

_____ Determine the questions you wish to have specifically addressed by references. Consider the areas of teaching, scholarship/artistic performance, citizenry/service, and preparation as an academician.

_____ A pool of semi-finalists is established.

EXERCISE

The scenario

Your recruitment committee has diligently screened candidates and worked hard to establish a group of semi-finalists. It now finds itself at loggerheads. The committee's teaching leader is assertively asking for inclusion of three candidates in the pool of semi-finalists with the scholarship leader vigorously disagreeing. The scholarship leader in turn wants two candidates to be named as semi-finalists who seem relatively weak in teaching. To make matters even more interesting, one member of the committee who was advocate for a candidate, is the only faculty who wants this applicant to be a semi-finalist.

As chair of the recruitment committee or one of its members, how do you proceed?

Some answers

It sounds as if the committee needs some cooling down, and it may want to take a break in its proceedings. Often tempers fray and focus is lost when the work load is heavy and people are tired. A break would allow the recruitment chairperson or another committee member to talk individually with colleagues and determine where the disagreements originate. This is when it is especially valuable if the committee has open communication among its members and is willing to openly thrash out differences. This committee seems to have members with differing opinions of what abilities a successful faculty should have.

To reiterate a major theme of this book, look at what would best serve your students, curriculum, and department. Get back to your selection criteria. Look at issues of fit. By focusing on what best serves students or the entire department, committee members can avoid losing face if their favorite candidates are removed from consideration. The committee needs to focus on a larger goal than its individual members' desires.

Finally, the committee can do some horse trading. The pool of 10 or so semi-finalists will have to be reduced to five finalists anyway. Perhaps the teaching and scholarship leaders can agree on one candidate each favors and a pool of 12 semi-finalists be established. Or other committee members can outvote both.

References and Recommended Readings

Boice, R. (1991). New faculty as teachers. *Journal of Higher Education, 62,* 150-173.

Boice, R. (1992). *The new faculty member: Supporting and fostering professional development.* San Francisco, CA: Jossey-Bass.

Davidson, C.I., & Ambrose, S. A. (1994). *The new professor's handbook: A guide to teaching and research in engineering and science.* Bolton, MA: Anker.

Deneef, A. L, Goodwin, C. D., & McCrate, E. S. (Eds.). (1988). *The academic's handbook.* Durham, NC: Duke University Press.

Gibson, G. W. (1992). *Good start: A guidebook for new faculty in liberal arts colleges.* Bolton, MA: Anker.

Marchese, T. J., & Lawrence, J. F. (1988). *The search committee handbook: A guide to recruiting administrators.* Washington, DC: American Association for Higher Education.

Sommerfield, R., & Nagely, D. (1974). Seek and ye shall find: The organization and conduct of a search committee. *Journal of Higher Education, 45,* 239-252.

Waggaman, J. S. (1983). *Faculty recruitment, retention and fair employment: Obligations and opportunities.* ASHE-ERIC Higher Education Research Report No. 2, Washington, DC: Association for the Study of Higher Education.

Zanna, M. P., & Darley, J. M. (Eds.). (1987). *The compleat academic: A practical guide for the beginning social scientist.* Hillsdale, NJ: Erlbaum.

11

IDENTIFYING FINAL CANDIDATES AND SELECTING CAMPUS VISITORS

You have ten semi-finalists who have been asked to provide teaching portfolios and videos of their teaching, and your committee members have developed their own preferences based on the credentials. What additional information do you need to select your finalists? What criteria in addition to those we have already discussed will you use to pick campus visitors?

We assume you have reduced your candidate pool to around ten semi-finalists. The task for the recruitment committee now becomes more difficult. Differences among remaining candidates are smaller, and any candidates dropped from consideration may be persons who would fit your position and work out well. The committee should be well-acquainted with its selection criteria by now, but it is often helpful to review them briefly at this point to refresh and improve your focus.

OBTAIN ADDITIONAL MATERIALS

Teaching Portfolios and Videotapes of Candidate Teaching

Part of the decision of whom to select as finalists and invite to your campus will be based on additional teaching information. Once semi-finalists have been selected, request a teaching portfolio and a videotape of their teaching to provide more information to assist in committee decision-making.

Give candidates a reasonable yet firm deadline for when you need these materials. The position description they already received should have indicated that these requests will be made of all semi-finalists, so they were forewarned. It is probably wise to remind candidates of these submissions as you communicate with them throughout the selection process.

Chapter 6 describes the nature of the teaching portfolio and the advantages of its use as a source of information on teaching philosophy and skills. The portfolio we suggest is not lengthy, but it is sufficient to provide some real insight into the teaching philosophy, experience, and classroom potential of each candidate.

The videotape will give you a good impression of candidates' teaching skills and personality in the classroom or studio and will be helpful in assessing pedagogic and interpersonal strengths. Be careful not to use a videotape to screen illegal or unethical criteria. The use of a rating form with standard categories to evaluate both the portfolio and the tape will help committee members to be objective.

Additional Scholarship Materials

You may request additional materials related to scholarship. If candidates have sent a sampling of their published work, ask for all of it if not too extensive. You may also want to read copies of grant proposals.

Telephone Calls to Semi-Finalists

As you narrow the semi-finalist pool to a list of the most promising candidates, it becomes more important to establish a personal contact with each of the remaining applicants and to gain fuller information to better judge their fit for your position. Telephone calls by recruitment committee members are often used for these purposes. Be sure to determine in advance if recruitment committee members can call from home and be reimbursed. This will allow calls to be made or returned in the evening, when both candidate and committee member have more opportunity for a relaxed exchange of information. Make sure that recruitment committee members identify times they are available for return calls and that your secretary has this information. If your university is equipped, consider a teleconferencing call to each candidate. Being able to see candidates when conversing assists in getting to know them and in assessing their abilities and potential.

Listen closely to candidates. You are looking for a level of comfort, honesty, responsibility, and maturity from them. Do candidates ask questions tactfully? Or is there a sense of entitlement in their responses? Candidates should be prepared to answer the types of questions presented below. Be sure to follow up if you have further questions about a response, and try to make the candidate feel comfortable in doing the same.

Have Goals in Mind When Calling

Before your committee makes phone calls, create a form with some common questions that each candidate will be asked. To prepare for questions which candidates may ask, we suggest that you survey your colleagues, especially new ones, and identify the questions that candidates might pose which would be most difficult to answer. What questions do they wish they had asked, and what information did they find most informative? Provide this information during your call. Be sure that you know something about your colleagues' professional interests and backgrounds in case you are asked. Some goals when making telephone calls include:

- Create an interest in and good feelings about your position.

- Communicate positive aspects of the position including information about the nature of your department, number of other untenured faculty, available facilities, the nature of undergraduate and/or graduate education offered, teaching load, and varieties of support available including space and equipment.

- Emphasize teaching responsibilities, including the specific classes you need taught.

- Describe anything else a candidate might be interested in, such as a strong teaching excellence center, good support for scholarship, unique calendar, the community, local schools.

- Describe your recruitment process (e.g., current status, visits, timetable on decisions).

- Be honest, but not defensive. For example, if candidates ask what recent pay raises have been, tell them, even if they have been low.

Sample Questions for Telephone Interviews

- Degree status. If PhD is not finished, what is the timetable?

- Teaching experience, interests, and requirements (e.g., equipment)?

- Research or artistic performance interests and requirements (space and equipment)?

- Describe the person who has been the biggest influence on your interest in teaching.

- Describe the person who has been the biggest influence on your motivation to do scholarship or perform artistically.

- Ask any questions about the materials in the candidate's file.

- Interest and motivation for coming to this department, institution, and community?

- What opportunities are sought here?

- Request any missing application materials.

- What questions or concerns does the candidate have?

Calling People Not Listed as References

In narrowing the pool, calls to people who know the candidate but are not listed as a reference, such as a department chair, are sometimes beneficial. For experienced candidates being considered for tenure or associate or professorial rank, some recruitment committees ask their department chair or dean to make a boss-to-boss call. Be sure candidates give their permission, since some may not want it known they are job hunting.

Dual-Career Couples

As the field of candidates is narrowed and phone calls are made, the issue of dual-career couples may arise. While candidates do not have to disclose their marital status, those with spouses or significant others having their own careers will usually inquire about employment opportunities either within the university or in the community. For spouses who will work in a different profession or discipline, find someone familiar with the employment situation in that field who can be their contact and provide useful information about local opportunities.

NARROWING THE FIELD: SELECTING FINALISTS

It is now time for what may be your longest recruitment committee meeting, so find a quiet location with pleasant surroundings. We recommend that you select approximately five finalists for the position. Decide if you need rules for this meeting, for example, we will not leave this room until we have five finalists. Some committees find that this meeting progresses relatively smoothly. Their working relationship, the nature of the applicant pool, and the selection criteria all lend themselves to relatively easy choices.

For other search committees, however, this meeting is difficult. Tensions between and among committee members, difficult choices between candidates, and multiple selection criteria all compete with each other and muddy the waters. This is when the committee chairperson's leadership is important. Committee members must be kept focused on the task at hand, and oftentimes feelings must be managed. No one committee member should be given the power to blackball any one candidate nor by themselves place someone in the finalist group (Marchese & Lawrence, 1988). Your decisions should be based on your selection criteria, and maintaining this focus will simplify the process.

Some committees begin by having members individually rank candidates in priority order and then sum the ranks. These rankings often help in reaching an early consensus on those who are clearly favored as finalists and others who can be dropped from consideration.

As already noted, if the job market or nature of the position is such that you cannot assume that one of the top two or three candidates will accept the position if offered, keep several candidates in a reserve pool and so inform them. But eventually, in whatever ways work best, the recruitment committee must identify a group of finalists. If you are unfortunate enough to reach a total impasse, you may have to invite others in your department to help with the choices. Often this problem can be solved, at least temporarily, by adding another candidate or two to the final list.

SELECTING CAMPUS VISITORS

Once approximately three to five finalists are identified, the committee must decide who will be invited for campus visits to allow you to further assess the candidates, and them to assess you. We recommend inviting no more than two or at most three candidates. We know of departments where five candidates are brought in for interviews, but the work and cost usually exceed the benefits gained.

Selecting the finalists who will make campus visits is relatively easy if two of the candidates are clearly the best choices. In other cases, however, the top five or six candidates are all impressive. In this situation the recruitment committee has to focus on the selection criteria—who is the best fit, who is most likely to accept a position if offered, and perhaps who is most likely to be retained. These are some of the same criteria used to decide whom to offer a position after campus visits (see Chapter 13). The decisions may be agonizing, and more telephone calls may be needed.

Another scenario involves five or six finalists who are all average. We agree with Waggaman's (1983) recommendation that you invite the best of the average in such cases. After seeing how this candidate fares during the visit, you can decide whether or not to offer a contract, look at other candidates, or reopen the search (see Chapter 13).

For pools with good finalists, we recommend bringing in at least two of your most promising candidates prior to a final hiring decision to allow a comparison between them. Given two candidates whose credentials on paper make them nearly equally good fits for the position, there is probably at least a 40% to 50% chance you will prefer the one ranked second over the original preference after you have met them, seen them teach, and attended a colloquium or artistic performance. After selecting two or three candidates for campus visits, the remaining candidates should be informed that while they have not been chosen for initial campus visits, they are still being actively considered. Keep in mind that you may move down your list of candidates, depending on whether you decide to offer one of the initial campus visitors the job, and whether they accept your offer.

Some final advice. Before asking your department or dean for campus visit permission, phone or e-mail each of your choices to determine if they are still available and interested in your position. It is embarrassing to receive permission to bring in a visitor who has already accepted another position. And make sure you have reviewed the tapes of the candidate teaching and performing before he or she comes for a campus visit. Seeing candidates teach and perform on video will suggest comments and questions to share with them.

Checking Credentials

Your committee has another decision to make at this point. How thorough does it want to be in substantiating important qualifications of finalists? Does it want to appoint someone to check credentials? We have never seen systematically gathered data on the veracity of applicants' credentials, but some faking, fraud, or at least resumé enhancement must occur. Do you want to verify degrees earned? In some cases an important piece of information, if you can get it, is the candidates' present job status. We all know of individuals who have been promised strong letters of support and recommendation if they "choose to leave" their present employment. You may also want to substantiate the list of publications. Asking for course syllabi helps substantiate teaching experience, yet syllabi are easily obtained and it is simple to put one's name on another's work.

You can talk with writers of recommendations or others familiar with the candidate's work, but be careful when checking references. Some candidates may not want their present employer to know they are job-seeking. You may need to talk with the applicant about how to proceed, although this may restrict your information gathering.

To our knowledge, most academic units do not do extensive checking of credentials beyond official transcripts. We recommend that if you have any questions in this area, you get them answered prior to offering a contract. While post-hiring revelations may add excitement to your recruiting experience, recruitment is not so much fun that you want to do it again soon.

Presenting Decisions on Campus Visits

Unless the recruitment committee has sole power to hire, which would be unusual, it must seek the approval of the department and/or dean before candidates are brought to campus. Prepare a summary of the recruitment process to date in the form of a brief presentation including the search criteria, the number of candidates making each cutoff, and other relevant information. End with a brief description of each finalist, a comparative evaluation, reasons for recommending specific individuals for campus visits, and a proposed budget for visits. Such a summary does not take a great deal of time to prepare but puts a great deal of organized information before whoever must make decisions on campus visits. This presentation also will convey the impression that your committee is well-organized and knows what it is doing, and it will give your recommendations more weight and credibility.

CHECKLIST

_____ Teaching portfolios are evaluated.

_____ Videotapes of semi-finalists' teaching and artistic performances are solicited and evaluated.

_____ Goals of telephone calls are established, and calls made.

_____ Pool of finalists is identified.

_____ Campus visit decisions (who, how many) are made.

_____ Finalists are contacted to determine if they are still available and are still interested in the position.

_____ Brief presentation of decisions and rationale for finalists and campus visitors is prepared.

The scenario

The position is tenure line at the assistant professor level. The committee has screened over 90 applications, read cover letters, vitae, teaching and research statements, and letters of recommendation, and it has made phone calls to candidates. Selection criteria include a balance of teaching and scholarship abilities and a candidate who has a good chance of being retained. The committee did not ask for teaching portfolios nor did they request videotapes of candidates teaching.

The search committee brings five finalists to a department meeting with two designated for campus visits. As a member of the department, you are asked to read the five sets of credentials in preparation for a meeting to discuss recommending the top two to the dean for visits. You review the files and find that the teaching criterion has been given little weight in deciding who will be invited.

- *What are some simple things you can do to ensure a careful discussion and decision on whom to invite?*

- *How can you be most helpful to your recruitment committee colleagues?*

Some answers

Start by making no assumptions. Your colleagues on the committee have been slogging through credentials for weeks. Your fresh eye gives perspective and new viewpoints to what candidates say. Consider all major areas of selection. Read about candidates' scholarship, citizenry and service, and teaching, and talk with committee members before the meeting. In this case, the committee's decisions regarding scholarship and interpersonal skills were validated. Scholarship of the top candidates was an excellent fit with what students and faculty desired. All finalists appeared to have potential to be excellent department citizens.

Focus on teaching. One department faculty noticed that she could not list the courses taught for Candidate A, one of the top two candidates. The committee members had confused courses this candidate wished to teach with past teaching experience; actual experience was less.

At the urging of another department member, the recruitment committee asked the top two candidates for additional teaching materials. These proved to be an eye-opener. Candidate A was teaching a course with a limited syllabus, and it turned out this was not a three-credit, full-semester course as had been believed. This led to a discussion of how well-prepared Candidate A was for the work of full-time teaching, why over time he had not availed himself of teaching opportunities, whether his expectations fit the position to be filled, and whether his credentials had been presented in an ethical fashion. In talking with the candidate about these issues, however, they were not as problematic as initially believed.

Another department member was concerned about Candidate B, an applicant just finishing a doctorate. What was the nature of the prestigious laboratory course he was teaching? It turned out that the syllabi and examinations were expertly written, the course was highly rigorous, and while this younger candidate had somewhat limited teaching experience, it appeared he was prepared for the rigors of developing several new courses if hired.

Reading the credentials also revealed that Candidate A's teaching philosophy emphasized class participation and discussion, but it was unclear how this strategy was implemented in the classroom. Again, in talking with Candidate A it became apparent that his teaching style was a well-considered mix of lecture and discussion. Candidate B seemed more comfortable with a lecture format in his teaching. This differentiation gave the department another dimension on which to compare the candidates' teaching credentials.

From a teaching perspective, the recruitment committee members had not done a thorough job. If they had done their homework and properly weighed and attended to teaching as a primary criterion in hiring, last minute information gathering and phone calls to the candidates would not have been necessary. Positively, both candidates came to campus with the department better prepared to appreciate their potential.

REFERENCES AND RECOMMENDED READINGS

Boice, R. (1991). New faculty as teachers. *Journal of Higher Education, 62,* 150-173.

Boice, R. (1992). *The new faculty member: Supporting and fostering professional development.* San Francisco, CA: Jossey-Bass.

Davidson, C.I., & Ambrose, S. A. (1994). *The new professor's handbook: A guide to teaching and research in engineering and science.* Bolton, MA: Anker.

Deneef, A. L, Goodwin, C. D., & McCrate, E. S. (Eds.). (1988). *The academic's handbook.* Durham, NC: Duke University Press.

Gibson, G. W. (1992). *Good start: A guidebook for new faculty in liberal arts colleges.* Bolton, MA: Anker.

Marchese, T. J., & Lawrence, J. F. (1988). *The search committee handbook: A guide to recruiting administrators.* Washington, DC: American Association for Higher Education.

Sommerfield, R., & Nagely, D. (1974). Seek and ye shall find: The organization and conduct of a search committee. *Journal of Higher Education, 45,* 239-252.

Waggaman, J. S. (1983). *Faculty recruitment, retention and fair employment: Obligations and opportunities.* ASHE-ERIC Higher Education Research Report No. 2, Washington, DC: Association for the Study of Higher Education.

Zanna, M. P., & Darley, J. M. (Eds.). (1987). *The compleat academic: A practical guide for the beginning social scientist.* Hillsdale, NJ: Erlbaum.

12

THE CAMPUS VISIT

What will your goals be for the candidates' campus visits? What do you want to learn that you do not already know? What impression will visiting candidates leave the campus with after they visit you? What about your department might be unusual or different? With whom should the candidate meet? Will you allow time for familiarization with the community?

The purposes of campus visits are to add to your knowledge about candidates, to provide data on their personal dimensions, to allow them to get to know you and your campus, and to woo them and they you. Campus visits often solidify decisions and choices already made, but on occasion they reveal poor fits between candidate and position or highlight personal traits (extreme shyness, strong personal attitudes) which may make excellent teaching and scholarship problematic. They also may point out department problems and issues which might make candidates hesitant to accept an offer, should one be made.

There is another, secondary goal of campus visits. You will be hiring again in the future, and positive experiences leave good impressions with candidates and others with whom they speak. Be professional, ethical, warm, and organized. Honesty and candor are good policies which minimize the raising of false expectations. A good working rule is that we should treat candidates making a campus visit as though we will encounter them later in our careers (Boice, 1992).

There is much to be done during a campus visit, so do not even consider having two candidates on campus at the same time. Each candidate deserves your focused attention. If you want a first-rate candidate to be interested in your position, you must run a first-rate campus visit. What follows is designed to help you do this.

CONTACTING THE CANDIDATE

While candidates will need time to make travel plans, prepare a colloquium and guest lecture, and ensure that work-related matters are covered in their absence, the recruitment must proceed in a timely fashion. We suggest that candidates make a campus visit about 2 weeks after your invitation. This allows you time to prepare their itinerary, and gives them sufficient time as well. Some candidates will be able to visit sooner; if possible, accommodate them. If a candidate, for whatever reasons, cannot visit your campus for several weeks, you may have to delete this applicant from consideration.

Prior to a campus visit, ask the candidate if there are any special circumstances which need to be identified, such as dietary preferences. Similarly, if a candidate is disabled, this needs to be known so that appropriate arrangements can be made. There are several elements which must be properly planned and executed to achieve the campus visit experience you want. We will consider these below.

MEET WITH THE DEPARTMENT

Prior to a campus visit, meet with the department to describe what is about to happen. Let your colleagues know who is being invited for a visit, tell them where a candidate's application materials are located, and ask them to review the position description. Impress on them the importance of reviewing these materials if they are meeting with the candidate. A few words about use of the interview and avoiding inappropriate questions will help to ensure that the visit goes well.

SEND MATERIALS IN ADVANCE OF A VISIT

Provide the candidate with as much information as possible describing the department, campus, and community in advance of the visit. This information makes for a more informed visitor who is better prepared to ask meaningful questions. Ask candidates if there are any materials which would be especially helpful for them. Table 12.1 lists a variety of materials describing the department and its programs, the university, and community. As you can see, the amount of information that could be sent is extensive. Choose those items you wish to send and mail this information to candidates as soon as you know who you will invite. Typically the itinerary is sent separately and last, as it is the final piece of information to be developed.

TABLE 12.1

INFORMATION TO SEND CANDIDATES PRIOR TO A CAMPUS VISIT

Departmental

- The college/university catalog with departmental undergraduate and graduate programs highlighted
- Other departmental program descriptions
- A list of faculty, academic backgrounds, professional interests, etc.
- Information on quality and backgrounds of undergraduate and graduate students
- Materials used to recruit students
- Photos and layouts of laboratories and studios
- Information on library holdings, and films and videotapes for your discipline
- A list of equipment provided to new hires (e.g., computer, phone, e-mail hookup)
- Department and university Renewal and Tenure Guidelines, and department By-Laws (if relevant)

College/University/State System

- Overview of the state system, if one exists for public institutions, and is relevant
- General campus information and maps
- Information on fringe benefits
- A description of faculty development and grant opportunities and support

- Sabbatical information
- Information on your institution's Teaching Excellence Center
- Mentoring program information
- A copy of any available video of the campus (such as those for student recruitment)
- A copy of the student newspaper
- Copies of union contracts (if relevant)
- Patent and copyright policy statements (if relevant)
- Consulting policy (if relevant)

Community

- Chamber of Commerce and Visitor's Bureau's materials including a video of the community (strongly recommended)
- Housing opportunities and costs
- Recent Sunday edition of the city's newspaper
- General cost of living information
- Career opportunities for spouses
- Cultural opportunities, and nearby colleges and universities
- Any other useful information

Other

- Reimbursable campus visit expenses and reimbursement procedure
- Copy of Itinerary

LODGING

A motel or hotel in a nice part of the city, and as near as possible to the university and airport, is usually desirable. You might consider arranging for a bowl of fruit or something similar for the candidate, and/or a small local gift (in our case an Oshkosh By-Gosh Bandanna). You do not have to spend a lot of money to make a visit to your campus pleasantly memorable, and the gesture will generate good feelings on both sides. If your campus has acceptable on-campus visitor housing, consider these accommodations.

USE OF TIME AND SCHEDULING

Your goal is a pleasant and smoothly organized campus visit which allows candidates to learn everything they want to know about the job and the community, and you to learn what you need to know about them. Begin planning for these visits as early as possible, giving careful consideration to the question of how to best use the time during the visit. The length of the visit is influenced by a variety of factors, some not under anyone's control. We recommend a visit of at least two days, and preferably three. This does not mean three complete days, but does ensure that time for travel, arrival, and departure will not occupy more time than the visit.

Survey faculty and class schedules to identify the best times for guest lectures, artistic performances, and/or presentation of colloquia, master classes, and recitals. You want to maximize attendance at these presentations, and you may wish to consider strategies to encourage students and faculty to come. We recommend that you make announcements in your classes, put up posters, use e-mail, and work hard at getting students (and faculty) to attend the colloquium, artistic performances, and guest teaching. Some arm twisting may be necessary. The recruitment committee must be active and assertive in asking colleagues and students to spend time with candidates. Part of the candidates' impression of your department is based upon the interest shown by faculty and students.

Campus Visit With Spouse Attending

On occasion, candidates will ask if their spouse (or significant other) can accompany them during a campus visit. Say yes. The candidate usually pays for these travel expenses, however. Spouses typically make a campus visit when quality of life, schooling for children, or career and job opportunities for the spouse are paramount. It is difficult to hire or retain new faculty when spouses have negative feelings or unanswered questions about living or working in your community. The best decision will be made if the spouse has complete information, and a visit to campus helps ensure this.

Your recruitment committees may want to extend an invitation to a candidate's spouse, if you know he or she is married. If a spouse makes a visit, someone on the recruitment committee or a spouse of someone in the department typically volunteers to provide this person information and give a tour of the community, helping the candidate's husband or wife learn about housing, schools, job opportunities, and the like.

The Shadow

Each candidate must have a department member who is available to help throughout the visit, typically a recruitment committee member. This host makes introductions, takes care of coats and briefcases, helps the candidate find rooms on campus, drops the candidate off at lodging at the end of the day, and generally is charged with making the details of the visit as pleasant and unobtrusive as possible. This task may be shared by two or more people. As noted, a spouse who visits campus also should be provided with a shadow.

Some recruitment committees ask the shadow to make a follow-up call to the candidate a few days after the visit to see that the person returned home safely, that everything went well, and to see if there is any information the shadow can provide. The shadow in this case is viewed as a friendly link (not an advocate) between the candidate and the formal search process.

Avoid Improper Questions

Take care not to ask improper questions at any time during a campus visit, but especially in social settings when doing so seems more appropriate. An interview dinner is not an occasion to question candidates about their marital status, sexual preference, race, age, or health (unless job-related). Questions must be job-related and those attending such dinners should be so informed.

LEARNING ABOUT THE DEPARTMENT, UNIVERSITY, AND COMMUNITY

Always Have a Printed Campus Visit Itinerary

To best organize a campus visit, make up a printed itinerary after you have arranged all meetings and presentations. A detailed itinerary helps the recruitment committee to anticipate problems in the campus visit. If time allows, share a draft copy of the itinerary by telephone or e-mail with candidates for their feedback. Some rules for a good itinerary include:

- Make sure everyone meeting with the candidate receives a copy as well as the candidate, and have extra copies printed (some will be misplaced).

- Include the names and titles of everyone the candidate is scheduled to meet, including all participants in group interviews. A few notes about the people whom the candidate will meet are useful. This is especially important information about people not in the department with whom the candidate will be speaking.

- List the room number of each meeting so candidates can find their own way if necessary.

- Arrange for someone to escort the candidate from one meeting to the next (often the shadow), and list these names in the itinerary.

- Do not leave the colloquium, course lecture, or audition for the end of the campus visit. The candidate is likely to be so tired and/or anxious that you will not learn what you wanted.

- Talk with the candidate about preference for a morning or afternoon guest lecture and colloquium.

- When in doubt, put in extra free time. Schedules run late, and candidates will appreciate a little time for themselves. Campus interviews are stressful, and there is a tendency to schedule something for every available minute. Allow time for rest, exercise, and preparation for presentations. You do not want to have to help candidates up the stairs to the airplane when they leave.

- Do not assume that printed material sent to a candidate is a substitute for firsthand knowledge. Candidates will want to meet with someone in the personnel and grants offices, even if they have received written information.

- Last, make sure to schedule activities that candidates suggest, such as a look at local housing options.

The tenet of full information applies to campus visits. Provide a brief sketch of candidates for those faculty or administrators meeting with them who are outside the department; a one page vitae usually works fine.

If the candidate will have group meetings while on campus, either with faculty, and/or with students, the recruitment committee should arrange for a chairperson for each meeting. The chair's job is to keep the meetings on track, to minimize bullying or inappropriate questions, and to discourage any strong personalities from monopolizing the conversation.

INTRODUCING THE DEPARTMENT

We suggest that the candidates be met at the airport and taken to their lodging by one person, preferably the committee chair or shadow. A meal with the chair and one or two others might follow. This will allow a low key introduction to the faculty most centrally involved in the search, and provide opportunities to review the candidate's schedule and answer initial questions. All meetings including meals are working sessions. We do not recommend arranging large social gatherings with department faculty and spouses. Have one of these early in the first semester your new colleague is with you. There is little if any down time during a visit. Even informal walks on campus with a candidate and other unstructured conversations communicate important information.

Have the candidate meet the departmental faculty individually or in small groups. A mass meeting of a large department or interest group may be useful after both sides have become acquainted in early meetings, but these large gatherings are unnecessarily stressful for the candidate if held shortly after their arrival, and often yield little useful information for either the candidate or the faculty.

There are usually a number of meetings between the candidate and various elements of the department. Those involved often include:

- The recruitment committee
- The department chair
- Interest group and/or department faculty
- Graduate students
- Undergraduate students including club or honorary society members

The Colloquium

Colloquia allow opportunities to see candidates at their best. Typically dissertation or ongoing research is material the candidate knows better than anything else. The content of the colloquium, its intellectual level, knowledge of the scholarly literature, and the nature and quality of the scholarship are important. Other factors of interest include the organization and clarity of presentation, the answering of questions, and ease before a critical audience in a difficult situation. Be sure to have the room and any necessary audio-visual (A-V) equipment reserved and ready to use.

Make sure the candidate knows who will be in the audience and the context in which the colloquium will be presented. Will it be made up of department faculty and students, or will faculty from other departments and administrators be invited? Of course you will tell the candidate the length of the colloquium, and how much of this time should be set aside for questions. Provide as much of this information as possible well in advance of the visit so proper preparation can be made.

The Artistic Performance or Audition

The artistic performance or audition requires the same preparation and communication of information as a colloquium. Typically a 30-minute audition presenting the performing artist's work is held for faculty and students. Reserve a period of time before the audition to allow the performer to collect thoughts and build the concentration necessary for an artistic presentation.

Teaching

Now is not the time to forget about a candidate's teaching abilities, potential, and responsibilities if hired. The committee's teaching leader may need to exercise leadership as a campus visit itinerary is developed. Candidates should:

Teach a class. We recommend one presentation in an introductory course, if possible. Allow the candidate to pick the content area. If it dovetails with an ongoing course, have the candidate guest lecture. If not, have the candidate, with students invited and present, deliver a lecture on a mutually agreeable topic. Nothing helps you better understand how candidates teach than watching them do it. Be sure to find out in advance what A-V equipment is needed. Make sure you receive feedback from faculty and students who attend, either through use of a formal rating form or by sampling them for opinions and observations. Keep in mind that you are looking for both relative strengths and weaknesses. We know of one department that videotapes such lectures and requires that all recruiting faculty who were not present view it before the departmental meeting to decide if a contract should be extended.

In appropriate disciplines, have candidates teach a studio class or give a private lesson. Choose two or three students of varying artistic maturity for lessons and have faculty and students observe.

Talk about teaching. Sometime after the lecture, make sure faculty talk with candidates about how it went and what they would do differently next time. Some time with candidates during the visit should focus on their pedagogical abilities. You can ask candidates questions such as:

- How do you feel about your teaching experiences?

- What are your strengths and weaknesses in teaching?

- What plans do you have for improving your teaching?

Discuss teaching responsibilities if hired. One specific issue which must be attended to, usually in a meeting with the department or interest group chair, is what courses the candidate would teach during the first year (and what other duties would be assigned). Candidates need a clear understanding of the number of different course preparations they would have, how many of these courses would be taught consistently, semester after semester, and how much latitude exists for developing courses new to the department's curriculum in the candidate's area of interest. These may be areas the candidate wishes to negotiate.

INTRODUCING THE COLLEGE OR UNIVERSITY

There are a number of individuals outside your department who can provide useful information to a candidate. Be sure to ask for their impressions. Some recruitment committees use a simple two or three item rating form which is easily completed. Candidates may find it useful to meet with:

- The dean and other administrators

- The institution's grants officer

- The institution's personnel officer regarding fringe benefits

- Faculty in other departments if closely related in scholarship or other interests

- A representative of your institution's mentoring program

- A representative of your Teaching Improvement Center

A brief or more extended tour of the campus should be arranged as time allows, emphasizing the facilities of most interest to the candidate. This experience will provide a broader picture of the campus community. Be sure to ask if candidates would like some time to walk around campus by themselves. Sometimes it is helpful to let them wander where they wish. The candidate might like to attend a concert or a sporting event, but do not force such scheduling. Their days are long and stressful, and many are ready to collapse at day's end.

An important consideration involves women or minority candidates. If there is a women's or minority caucus or interest group on campus, candidates from these groups may want to schedule a meeting with a representative. By meeting privately with other women or minorities they may feel less isolated, and gain valuable information on the university, department, and community. The same principle applies to males in a predominantly female discipline.

Introducing the Community

Candidates, especially those with a family, will want some introduction to the community. Again, send as much information as possible prior to the visit. Ask candidates if there is any specific information related to hobbies they would like to receive. While you are interviewing someone about a job opening, remember that not all of life involves work. Someone who sails may be very interested in your position because of its proximity to water. The same principle holds true for candidates with other hobbies such as skiing, music, or running.

Have someone who is knowledgeable about the community volunteer to take candidates around town or show them several residential areas. Many candidates are interested in and concerned about where they might live. If you know the candidate's preferences (urban housing, rural housing, rental, or purchase), you can be prepared to make best use of the time. Expect to spend a minimum of two to three hours introducing the community.

Reimbursement

Candidates will expect to have their basic expenses reimbursed, and those who are just finishing their degrees will probably appreciate having this matter dealt with promptly. If forms for travel, food, and/or lodging must be filled out, designate someone (possibly your departmental secretary) to be responsible for this, and put this item on the candidate's schedule. We suggest having the proper forms prepared in advance with name, address, purpose for visit, and other required information already filled in. Provide examples of completed forms, a list of everything a candidate must attach (e.g., last copy of plane ticket, receipts of various types), and a stamped addressed envelope for mailing it to campus. You might suggest that the candidates complete the form on the plane while flying home and mail it when they arrive. (The danger of this procedure is that the candidate may come to expect that all business functions on your campus are equally well-organized.)

Important Information For and From the Candidate

Whether or not candidates inquire, and we recommend that candidates be encouraged to ask for important information, there are a number of very practical items that should be discussed prior to or during the visit, so finalists are fully informed. These include the following:

- The number of candidates who have been and will be invited to visit before a decision is made
- When the candidate will be notified of a decision
- Who will discuss salary and what an approximate beginning salary is
- If an offer will be made during the visit—when, and by whom
- If an offer is made, how much time the candidate has to respond
- How salary raises are determined and the pattern of salary increases in recent years
- Whether and how previous experience is computed toward rank and tenure
- The standard initial contract length and renewal period
- Job responsibilities including courses to be taught, expectations for scholarship or performance, and service to the department and institution

Discussion of these items will avoid many potential misunderstandings and make for a productive visit. Open communication is always advisable, and there is no reason that any of these items should be considered awkward or embarrassing. Candidates will be much more comfortable if they know what to expect, and how to interpret various actions.

An important piece of information for the recruitment committee and department is how soon candidates believe they can respond if offered a contract. This is a fair question and one which should be asked. We also recommend that a direct question be posed about whether the candidate has made or will make other campus visits and/or has been offered a contract somewhere else. Such questions put the candidate on the spot, but may be central to how the recruitment proceeds. Such a question is best asked near the end of the campus visit by the chair of the recruitment committee. Be diplomatic, and assure the candidate that your interest is only to predict the potential timeliness of a response after an offer is made.

Other important information includes the current status of the candidate's dissertation if it is not yet completed, and where the candidate can be reached after the visit. This information is especially important if candidates will be attending a national conference or meeting. Can they be reached there or do they have an answering machine at home or work they will check? At this stage of the recruitment process, it is critical not to lose several days in obtaining critical information from a candidate or in making an offer.

OTHER CAMPUS VISIT ISSUES

Be Consistent, Fair, and Professional

The onus of consistent, structured, ethical behavior falls on those recruiting. The number of horror stories academic candidates can tell about campus visits seems endless. Avoid actions like the following:

- Calling candidates by the wrong name

- Impressing candidates with your commitment to teaching and then not allowing them to teach a class during the visit

- Advertising for a three-year temporary position and telling candidates it has become a one-year position when they come for interviews, or when the job is offered

- Asking candidates to prepare a talk geared toward students and then have your departmental faculty and dean at the presentation, but few students

- Changing the itinerary in any major way without the candidate's knowledge

The Unexpected

Campus visits are variations on a theme; structured and similar, yet each one somewhat different. Do not be surprised if each candidate makes at least one request you had not expected. For example, candidates may ask if a second visit is possible if a job offer is tendered, so that they can better make up their mind. We are aware of candidates who made special dietary preferences known after arriving on campus, and others who came and then informed the committee they had to leave a day early.

A good campus visit requires a lot of work and some luck. Nonetheless, something will go wrong. We guarantee it. Travel and weather can be particular problems. Having candidates visit our campus in late spring with snow on the ground is interesting for them if they are from warmer climates. It is less attractive when we have a late spring storm, the plane is hours late, and there are 10 inches of new snow with more falling. Even if the weather is perfect, plane flights may still be late. Have contingency plans.

Once a candidate reaches campus, glitches will occur—the piece of laboratory apparatus the candidate is interested in will break, the computer network will be down, or the two graduate students most interested in doctoral work with the applicant will both have the flu. We have just not learned how to appease the god or goddess of campus visits.

The Disastrous Campus Visit

On occasion, a campus visit is a disaster. Candidates may be sick and get worse, or they may become ill after they arrive. We are aware of one campus visit where the applicant was so sexist that the department knew within two hours that completing the itinerary was only going through the motions. Yet they did so. Despite doing their homework, this facet of the candidate was a surprise. Remember that one of the reasons for a visit is to discover problems such as this prior to offering a contract. In a sense, this visit was a "success."

In these situations common sense must prevail. If candidates are ill, the first priority is their comfort and health. Leave it up to them if they feel able to proceed with job-related meetings and business. Give them your full support and permission to leave early to return home and to return the next week, if possible, once well. If the recruitment is under very tight time or financial constraints, the candidate may need to be informed that a return visit to campus is not possible. While disappointing, this is honest communication. You will just have to make your decision based on the information you already have on the candidate.

A Take-Home Package

A take-home package, sometimes called an airplane package, for each candidate can be useful. Consider a copy of the student or city newspaper, a copy of a speech the president or chancellor made at Convocation, or anything which reinforces the positive aspects of the visit. Keep selling. Candidates will do the same. Thoughtful candidates will write a note to the recruitment committee chairperson upon returning home thanking everyone for their hospitality and courtesy during their visit.

CHECKLIST

_____ Determined if more than one candidate can be invited.

_____ Package of materials to send visitors is prepared.

     _____ Department material

     _____ University material

     _____ Community material

_____ A shadow is identified.

_____ Lodging is arranged.

_____ Candidate is informed regarding reimbursement of expenses.

_____ Reimbursement forms are prepared.

_____ Questions regarding a contract offer, salary, and other matters are answered.

_____ Length and focus of colloquium or audition is decided, and best time for colloquium is identified.

_____ Teaching during the campus visit is arranged.

     _____ Candidate will teach a class

     _____ Other time to discuss teaching arranged

_____ Attendance at candidate's colloquium, teaching, and meetings with students is encouraged.

_____ Candidate has a clear understanding of the nature and expectations of the position.

_____ Campus visit itinerary is sent.

EXERCISE

The scenario

A recruitment committee has recommended two candidates to its department and dean for campus interviews. Each is well-qualified in terms of teaching experience and scholarship, and both seem promising departmental citizens. The recruitment committee is concerned, however, about its ability to recruit and retain a new faculty member because of problems within the department.

The department has two competing factions, each with senior and junior faculty, which differ in their vision of what the department should be and how it should be run. The previous occupant of the vacant position left in great disgust that the department, instead of focusing on its students and education, seemed to spend inordinate amounts of time on departmental politics and issues of influence. While this one faculty member has recently left, several others have stayed, and seem to like the department.

Up to this point, the recruitment committee has done an excellent job. Department problems were openly acknowledged, the recruitment committee has worked with its colleagues, and things seem to be settling down. Both candidates recommended for campus visits were unanimously approved by the department; although each faction has a different preference. There are no overt concerns regarding academic abilities or potential.

- *How would you proceed with the campus visits?*
- *How would you schedule the candidates' time?*

Some answers

The best solution to a situation such as this is a good planning process with action to resolve the problem situation prior to the recruitment. Failing this, or in addition to this, open and honest communication is your best fall-back position. You do not want to deceive candidates, have them accept the job, grow dissatisfied, and leave. You will just have to recruit again, and deal with the same problem once more. If candidates know what they are getting into, they are more likely to stay if hired.

Each candidate has a right to know about this situation before a campus visit. An open recruitment demands nothing less. At the same time, the recruitment committee needs to continue its work with colleagues on implications both within and outside the department if the internecine warfare is allowed to influence the recruitment.

The candidate should be given *carte blanche* to ask department faculty about these problems during the visit. If candidates wish to talk with their predecessor in the position, they should be allowed to do so. They should also be provided an opportunity to meet privately with the department's junior faculty who will be their untenured colleagues.

REFERENCES AND RECOMMENDED READINGS

Boice, R. (1992). *The new faculty member: Supporting and fostering professional development.* San Francisco, CA: Jossey-Bass.

Davidson, C.I., & Ambrose, S. A. (1994). *The new professor's handbook: A guide to teaching and research in engineering and science.* Bolton, MA: Anker.

Deneef, A. L., Goodwin, C.D., & McCrate, E. S. (Eds.). (1988). *The academic's handbook.* Durham, NC: Duke University Press.

Gibson, G. W. (1992). *Good start: A guidebook for new faculty in liberal arts colleges.* Bolton, MA: Anker.

Marchese, T. J., & Lawrence, J. F. (1988). *The search committee handbook: A guide to recruiting administrators.* Washington, DC: American Association for Higher Education.

Sommerfield, R., & Nagely, D. (1974). Seek and ye shall find: The organization and conduct of a search committee. *Journal of Higher Education, 45*, 239-252.

Waggaman, J. S. (1983). *Faculty recruitment, retention and fair employment: Obligations and opportunities.* ASHE-ERIC Higher Education Research Report No. 2, Washington, DC: Association for the Study of Higher Education.

Zanna, M. P., & Darley, J. M. (Eds.). (1987). *The compleat academic: A practical guide for the beginning social scientist.* Hillsdale, NJ: Erlbaum.

13

CONCLUDING THE SEARCH: HIRING, REOPENING, OR CLOSING

Are you happy with your finalists, and can they do the job you need done? What important information did you gain during the campus visit? How will your department decide who is offered the position, if anyone, and what criteria and procedures should be used?

Your last campus visitor has departed, and it is now time to decide who, if anyone, will receive an offer. While most of the search is behind you, some very important decisions and work lie ahead. The purpose of this chapter is to help you make the best decision you can—to either extend a contract, invite other finalists to visit, reopen, or cancel the search. We also will discuss the necessary administrative details if a position is offered and accepted.

SELECTING A NEW COLLEAGUE

A department or interest group meeting must be called to discuss the finalists and to reach a decision on offering a contract. We recommend that this meeting have no other agenda items. For a focused meeting and good decision-making, we recommend the following.

Keep Selection Criteria Clearly in Mind

It is interesting how many new variables are thrown into the selection hopper after finalists visit campus. Be careful: many of these new candidate dimensions are not especially (or legally) relevant to the selection process.

We recommend that the head of the search committee chair the department's meeting on extending a contract, and begin by presenting, again, a brief summary of the recruitment process, the selection criteria used, and the reasons the campus visitors were selected. Be specific. List the courses your new hire will be teaching and the type of scholarship or artistic performance needed. This information focuses department members on the task at hand, rather than on personality issues or other factors which may not be terribly relevant to good teaching, scholarship, artistic performance, or service potential.

Do not hire someone, no matter how well he or she teaches, does research, or performs, who will be unable to meet all criteria for contract renewal or tenure. While you want to secure top faculty, you also want to retain them. Candidates who are unlikely to meet your department's and university's scholarship requirements for tenure are a risky selection, regardless of how well they teach. We say this despite our emphasis on teaching in selection. Likewise, laboratory stars who cannot teach should be avoided.

Have Complete Information

The recruitment committee members should touch base with their colleagues before the department meeting to discuss impressions of the candidates. Make sure these brief interactions take place, and do not be surprised if you have to contact candidates with last minute questions as a result of these discussions. For example, someone may have heard that completion of the dissertation has been delayed. You will want to confirm or refute this before the department meets.

Bring all the data you have collected to the meeting. Have candidate folders and transcripts available so faculty members can skim them and so that emergent questions or misinformation can be clarified. Gather feedback from students who met the candidates, faculty from outside your department, and others who met with the visitors. Have the recruitment committee chair or a member of the committee briefly present all the data and feedback on each campus visitor. Then, throw the meeting open for discussion and debate. Make sure everyone in the department is heard. Whoever is chairing the meeting must ensure that the most vocal and the quietest have all spoken their mind.

Look for the Best Fit

You must once again evaluate issues of fit at this stage in the recruitment process. Assess factors related to a good fit using your selection criteria and those Boice (1992) identified after discussing recruitment with chairpersons. These include: (1) a match between interests of departmental faculty and those of the candidate, (2) someone who seemed genuinely interested in joining the department, (3) someone who was genuinely positive about visiting campus, and (4) someone who had good personal interactions during interviews.

The campus visit allows evaluation of the fit between the candidate and your faculty and students. Did particular candidates elicit questions and discussion from students when others did not? Did any of the candidates have such breadth and fit of interests that they connected with several different members of the department? Of particular interest is how candidates fit with the teaching interests and scholarship/artistic performance of the subspecialty faculty with whom they will work closely. Those faculty members who work with their new colleague on a daily basis have the most to gain or lose, and should be attended to carefully during your discussion.

Discuss Issues of Acceptance (and Retention)

Decisions on the person to receive an offer may hinge, in part, on guessing which candidates would accept an offer and stay once employed. If this information is important to the department, be assertive but fair in pressing candidates for answers.

Most candidates need time to respond to an offer. *The Ethics of Recruitment and Faculty Appointment* adopted by the Council of Colleges of Arts and Sciences (CCAS) in November, 1992, and jointly adopted by the American Association of University Professors (AAUP) in June, 1993 recommend giving candidates two weeks to respond (CCAS, 1992). Many offers are tendered during the same brief period each spring. If your first candidate is ambivalent or waiting to hear about another position, your second choice may accept an offer while you await the decision of the first. Even so, never pressure candidates into making premature decisions. Be prepared and know in advance how long you can await their decision. Let them reach their own decision. But do not give candidates inordinate amounts of time to make up their minds; two weeks should be plenty. If candidates try to hold you up unreasonably, you must assertively define the conditions of the offer and let them decide.

Leave the Meeting With a Decision

When all is said and done, you must leave this departmental meeting with a decision. Either you will offer someone the position, bring someone else in for a campus visit, or reopen the search during this academic year or next.

The department will have to vote on its preference on who, if anyone, should be offered a contract. In many cases this vote is unanimous, but in others a split vote results. We recommend that the chair use proper parliamentary procedure to suggest that a unanimous vote be entered in the minutes. Unless the discussion was unusually acrimonious this is easily accomplished, and it is nice to be able to tell the candidate the vote was unanimous. If more than one candidate is acceptable, we recommend that a second choice be identified, and possibly a third. The position can then be reoffered quickly if the first choice declines.

OFFERING THE POSITION

In many universities, the dean or provost tenders offers. Sometimes these administrators want supporting documentation describing why a certain candidate is being offered a position and others are not. Administrators will often telegraph in advance the types of candidates most acceptable to them. Be prepared with paperwork and arguments to support your decision.

When making an offer to the candidate, offer your congratulations, and convey your sincere interest. Inform the candidates of the exact nature of the position, general terms of employment, and how long they have to decide. Candidates often have important questions they need to resolve before they commit themselves. Be prepared for these questions, perhaps a second quickly-made campus visit alone or with a spouse, and some very specific questions about salary, moving costs, fringe benefits, start-up monies, and other important issues. Expect some negotiations to take place.

Telephone offers must be followed by written letters tendering an offer within 10 days of informally offering a position (CCAS, 1992). We recommend writing even more promptly. Suggested content for such letters is listed in Table 13.1, and it varies with institutional policy. Despite the amount of required content, try to personalize this letter. If your dean is writing the letter, use our suggested content to remind the dean of what the department believes is important to convey to the candidate.

The letter of offer constitutes a binding commitment and must be carefully written. Your department, college, and university will have established rules and protocols for who sends these letters and their content. CCAS (1992) guidelines say that no such letters should be sent to someone working at another college or university after May 1, and that no faculty member can resign after May 15 to pursue other academic appointments unless all parties concerned agree.

Keep Communication Timely and Open

There are a variety of letters to write and phone calls to make to campus visitors and other finalists. Remaining finalists will need to be contacted and told their exact status and your timetable. Campus visitors must be thanked for their time and interest in your position. Be honest and candid. You will not only create good will, but it is possible one of these finalists will eventually be offered the position.

TABLE 13.1

CONTENT OF A LETTER OF OFFER*

Terms

- Initial rank
- Whether appointment is tenure track
- Credit toward tenure and length of the probationary period
- Conditions of contract renewal
- Salary and benefits
- Duties (job description—expectations of teaching, research/artistic performing, service, etc.)
- Special institutional arrangements or commitments for start-up (e.g., laboratory space, reduced teaching load for first year)
- Other details of departmental and institutional policy which affect the appointment
- Appointment beginning and end dates
- Date work begins
- Date by which the candidate is expected to respond to the offer (not less than 2 weeks from its receipt)

Other Content

- Official position title and working title, if appropriate
- Percentage of appointment (e.g., full, 3/4)
- Need for a physical examination, if required
- Form of formal acceptance (e.g., separate letter, signing a copy of offer letter, or contract)
- Statement on meaning of tenure, if offered

- Statement on who must approve the appointment (e.g., Board of Regents or Trustees)

Special Situations

- Any statement or university policy on providing reasonable accommodations for disabled employees
- Required evidence of employment eligibility (e.g. immigration)
- Expectations for completion of doctoral work, if not yet completed
- Agreed date when doctoral work will be done
- Definition of completion (e.g., dissertation defended, degree conferred)
- Salary raise, if any, once dissertation completed
- Consequences if doctoral work not completed by agreed upon date (e.g., termination of employment)
- Temporary appointments
- Institutional statement on teaching responsibilities
- Description of enclosures (e.g. Faculty Handbook, personnel rules, procedures/expectations for contract renewal and tenure)

* Council of Colleges of Arts and Sciences Guidelines: The ethics of recruitment and faculty appointment. (1992). Columbus, OH: Author. The Ohio State University, 186 University Hall, 230 North Oval Mall, Columbus, OH 43210-1319. Approved by AAUP in 1993.

Keep Focused on Recruiting

These last few weeks are critical to the recruitment. Remain focused. Many candidates have been lost over a few hundred dollars of salary, moving expenses, or inability to purchase needed equipment. This loss makes little sense when you consider the time and cost which have gone into hiring the best possible person for the position, and that this may be a million dollar, long-term decision. If you have the resources or ability to meet the expectations of your number one candidate, do so.

OTHER SEARCH ALTERNATIVES: CONTINUING, REOPENING, CLOSING

You may need to choose between continuing the search and inviting more candidates for campus visits, expanding the pool of candidates by reposting the position and reopening the search either this academic year or next, or closing the search and losing the position.

Continuing the Search

If none of your campus visitors were acceptable or if they declined offers, the search goes on (and you may want to limit the recruitment chair's access to sharp or pointed objects). At this point in the recruitment process, you do not have to write a new position description or post new job announcements. Now your ethical treatment of candidates, open communication, candor, and honesty may pay off. While no one wants to be a second choice, your fifth or sixth ranked finalists will often be pleased to be offered an opportunity to meet with you.

If your finalists are all unavailable or unacceptable after campus visits, the recruitment committee must decide if the position as described is viable or flawed. If your position remains viable, perhaps you can still recruit successfully. What you must keep in mind is that you may have a perfectly acceptable position and salary, but were turned down because candidates chose other career options. Are there any high-ranking semi-finalists who have been kept in a pool for just this situation who can now be invited for campus visits, assuming they remain available and interested?

If so, the need for good documentation of the search becomes even more important. You must convince a dean or provost to fund a third or fourth visit. We recommend inviting one candidate at a time at this point, and offering the first acceptable candidate a contract.

Reopening the Search

Reopening a search involves a decision that a new or expanded pool of candidates must be established. Typically a search is reopened in one of two situations: (1) a viable position but insufficient candidates from whom to select, and (2) a flawed position. The first case means that existing position descriptions can be retained but that job announcements will have to be reposted. In the second situation, both a new position description and a new job announcement must be written.

A viable position—no suitable candidate. The position may be acceptable as defined and described, but few candidates exist to fill it. Yours may have been a search with only a few candidates available nationally, none of whom you could attract. This may have occurred because they obtained positions elsewhere, a matter of bad luck on your part. If time permits, move forward by reposting the job announcement and seeing who applies. If errors in recruitment such as insufficient advertising led to no suitable candidates and a need to reopen the position, try to avoid making these mistakes again.

A flawed position. Another possibility is that the position is inherently flawed. Finalists may have turned you down (or potential candidates may not have applied) because of serious problems with salary, the position requirements, or other structural elements in the position. Did the department and its recruitment committee misread the position? Is it less desirable than originally thought? If any of these are the case, it may be next to impossible to successfully fill the position as it is constituted, and you must consider restructuring the position and reopening the search. The recruitment committee will have to do more planning and a new position description must be written and new job announcements posted. If time permits, begin at once.

A critical factor in this decision is whether the position will be lost if recruitment is delayed until the following year. With so many institutions facing uncertain fiscal environments, the risk is high that some positions will be swept up if not filled. In this case it may be worthwhile to keep looking despite the late date, but assess this strategy carefully before proceeding. Boice (1992) observes that many regrettable decisions in hiring are marked, in part, by selecting a low-priority candidate rather than risking losing permission to hire. The negative consequences of hiring someone with whom you and your students will be unhappy are so severe that you must be willing to leave the position unfilled, and lose it if need be.

Working with administrators on valid needs such as additional salary takes time. It also takes time for job announcements to be republished, and the time requirements of another recruitment may push most reopened search efforts into the summer when few faculty (or candidates) are available.

If it is simply too late to engage in this additional planning and preparation, seek permission to reopen the search next year.

Reopening a search the next academic year. Sometimes stopping a search for the present and reopening it during the next academic year is the best choice. In this situation you may need to seek funds to hire a temporary part-time faculty member to fill in for a year. Paperwork and data which inform your dean of the effort and planning which went into the unsuccessful search may help in obtaining this permission.

The next year of recruiting should go smoothly. With most of the planning and committee work done, job announcements should be published in early fall with early campus visits to follow. The critical task is to make sure that the reasons you did not hire successfully the previous year have been identified and corrected.

Terminating a Search

Once in a while, despite good planning and hard work on the part of a recruitment committee, a search must be terminated. The fiscal situation may have worsened so the monies on which the search was contingent never materialized. Structural changes in your department or college may eliminate your reason to recruit. If it is necessary to call off the recruitment, good planning may assist the department in coping without the new position. In a case such as this, contact all remaining candidates and explain the situation honestly.

A CANDIDATE ACCEPTS: NOW WHAT?

When a candidate accepts your offer, there is still much to do. For example, make sure the candidate knows that only those legally responsible can approve a signed contract and inform him when this happens. This is almost always a matter of routine, but candidates may be nervous, and who can blame them until they are officially employed.

Complete Your Paperwork

Keep current on the status of the new hire's contract with your dean's and personnel office. Wrap up the recruitment committee's paperwork and file everything in an organized fashion. Have your new faculty member send exact specifications of equipment to be purchased with start-up funds and make sure all paperwork related to its purchase is completed and forwarded.

Assist New Hires With Their Teaching

To allow your new hires to plan their curricular work and to provide them with some stability, we recommend that they receive a written statement of what they will teach during their first two or three years, if possible. New course preparations are extremely time-consuming and to surprise a new hire with an unexpected course preparation may be unethical and an abuse of power. Should an emergency require a deviation from such plans, the need for revision will be apparent to all.

Provide copies of syllabi from the courses to be taught. If a text for certain courses has not been selected, and individual faculty members order books, provide examples of texts for consideration. Offer to have the department secretary call publishers and have texts and ancillary materials sent directly to the new hire or to your campus. Apprise book stores that orders for these courses may be late.

Prepare for Your New Colleague's Arrival

Retention of new colleagues starts with the simple things. Have their office cleaned and painted if necessary, and order a name plate for the door. Make sure a mailbox is assigned, phone connected, and keys to the building, mailbox, and laboratory are ready to give them. If a computer was ordered, try to have it in the office and working when the new colleague arrives.

Another part of retention is helping your new colleagues succeed during the difficult first year in an academic position. Urge them to arrive as early as possible to settle in and find their away around the campus and community, and put them in contact with other recently hired faculty for help in finding housing. Graduate or undergraduate students are often available to help in moving when the new hire arrives.

CHECKLIST

_____   Department meeting was held to recommend offering a contract.

      _____   Selection criteria clearly in mind

      _____   Complete information available

      _____   Looked for best fit

      _____   Discussed timetable for candidate acceptance

_____   Left meeting with a decision.

      _____   Candidate(s) identified to be extended an offer

      _____   Others informed of status

_____   Search alternatives are investigated, if needed.

      _____   Search continued

      _____   Search reopened this academic year

      _____   Search to be reopened next academic year

      _____   Search terminated

_____   Candidate accepted the position.

_____   Search paperwork completed.

_____   Recruitment committee celebration is underway.

EXERCISE

The scenario

A department had an open position for an associate professor to administer a graduate training program, in a market with few applicants. However, this position required national professional certification in the discipline. The recruiting department viewed this position requirement as necessary to meet its goal of improving graduate program quality. The teaching load for the position was four courses/semester.

By the middle of March, none of the three finalists who were offered the position had accepted.

- *How should the recruitment committee proceed?*

- *What would you focus on?*

Some answers

The committee reassessed the academic program and the position description. It concluded that the pool of candidates who had taken and passed the certification examination was small. Those certified were more likely to work at larger universities or in the private sector. In addition, the teaching load, while the same as for other faculty in the university, was perceived as high by candidates. Salary was competitive, but not outstanding. Positively, the graduate program was perceived as having potential by the candidates who had made campus visits. The position itself was tenure line, with nothing inherently wrong with it.

The committee made the decision to reopen the search the same academic year. While the dean was not willing to decrease the teaching load nor increase the salary, she did approve the department suggestion that the certification requirement be deleted, and that the rank be changed to assistant or associate professor. The committee had concluded that while certification of its program head would lend prestige to the graduate program, it would not necessarily increase the teaching, scholarly, or administrative potential or abilities of applicants. The dean's approval allowed the committee to consider several newer PhDs who had already applied for the position, stating in their cover letters that they wished to be considered even though they lacked certification. When new job announcements appeared, these and several excellent new applicants were ranked as finalists. Campus interviews took place in late spring and a program head was offered and accepted a contract.

REFERENCES AND RECOMMENDED READINGS

Boice, R. (1991). New faculty as teachers. *Journal of Higher Education, 62*, 150-173.

Boice, R. (1992). *The new faculty member: Supporting and fostering professional development.* San Francisco: Jossey-Bass.

Council of Colleges of Arts and Sciences. (1992). *The ethics of recruitment and faculty appointment.* Columbus, OH: Author.

Davidson, C.I., & Ambrose, S. A. (1994). *The new professor's handbook: A guide to teaching and research in engineering and science.* Bolton, MA: Anker.

Deneef, A. L, Goodwin, C. D., & McCrate, E. S. (Eds.). (1988). *The academic's handbook.* Durham, NC: Duke University Press.

Gibson, G. W. (1992). *Good start: A guidebook for new faculty in liberal arts colleges*. Bolton, MA: Anker.

McKeachie, W. J. (1994). *Teaching tips: Strategies, research, and theory for college and university teachers (9th ed.)*. Lexington, MA: D.C. Heath.

Marchese, T. J., & Lawrence, J. F. (1988). *The search committee handbook: A guide to recruiting administrators*. Washington, DC: American Association for Higher Education.

Ross, R. D. (1981, May). The fine art of faculty recruitment. *Music Educators Journal, 67*, 49-51.

Sommerfeld, R., & Nagely, D. (1974). Seek and ye shall find: The organization and conduct of a search committee. *Journal of Higher Education, 45*, 239-252.

Waggaman, J. S. (1983). *Faculty recruitment, retention and fair employment: Obligations and opportunities*. ASHE-ERIC Higher Education Research Report No. 2, Washington, DC: Association for the Study of Higher Education.

Zanna, M. P., & Darley, J. M. (Eds.). (1987). *The compleat academic: A practical guide for the beginning social scientist*. Hillsdale, NJ: Erlbaum.

14

RETAINING YOUR NEW HIRE

Think back to when you were a new faculty member. What were the things which caused you to stay in your first position or to seek greener pastures? What could your colleagues have done to make your adjustment to faculty life smoother? What will your department, college, or university do to maximize your new hire's satisfaction and productivity, and to improve your chance of retaining this person and avoiding another recruitment?

The recruitment is complete, or at least you would like to think so. But what is the point of all your work recruiting the best possible new faculty members if you then abandon them to their own devices? How can you help new hires cope with job stress, the newness of everything they will encounter, and the problems inherent in living in a new community? Efforts to retain newly hired colleagues are an often overlooked, but crucial part of recruitment.

"…support programs for new faculty make sense as institutional investment; the costs, both economic and human, of losing new hires to competitors or to unproductive and unhappy beginnings are clearly greater than those of setting up effective support programs." (Boice, 1992, p. xi)

The effort it would take to mentor a new colleague is less than the much larger amount of work to be done if a new colleague leaves, and another recruitment must be conducted. How many hours did you and your colleagues spend on this recruitment? It will take much less time to assist your new colleague.

SUCCESSFUL MENTORING AND GOOD RECRUITING

You cannot salvage poor recruiting with mentoring. You want both a sound recruitment and a good mentoring process in place.

We are all aware of departments and colleges that assume it is new faculty members' responsibility to find their own way through the maze of the professoriate—after all, we did. In such cases, no mentoring or a weak mentoring system exists and there is little effort to work with, advise, or assist junior colleagues. This wastes the time spent in recruiting someone, and creates for all faculty an uninviting culture in which to work.

Our goal in this chapter is to describe a variety of systematic steps that you can take to make your new hires feel at home and to assist them in becoming productive faculty members. We will discuss three factors which are important in retaining new faculty: (1) helping new hires cope with their development as faculty; (2) mentoring; and (3) providing points of entry to the campus and community.

DEVELOPMENTAL ISSUES

Boice (1992) provides a readable and concise description of new faculty development. He makes the point that learning to teach well is extremely difficult, partly because many new faculty spend too much time and effort on the wrong problems, such as what he terms defensive teaching skills (e.g., writing the perfect lecture) and not enough time developing broad-based academic skills such as balancing tasks within both academic and non-academic responsibilities. Examples include a balance between (1) lecturing and other facets of teaching; (2) teaching and other responsibilities, such as scholarly research and writing; and (3) socializing both on and off campus. Few find such balance on their own, but faculty who immerse themselves in campus activities over time are more successful teachers and scholars.

Help your new hires become productive faculty members, coping with or avoiding the problems Boice (1992) describes in the developmental process of many new faculty.

- The first year is marked by loneliness and little discussion of teaching, the expectation that other faculty will seek you out, generally negative feelings toward senior colleagues, and disappointed expectations.

- The second year provides some relief, although new faculty still feel like newcomers with even more pressure to do scholarship. The end of the second year brings a new low, with feelings of social isolation and intellectual under-stimulation. Generally those with mentoring feel acceptance; those without do not. Things get worse before they get better; new faculty feel overwhelmed in their second year before their situation improves in the third.

- In the third year, new faculty cope better, with some finding social support, usually from colleagues. Many remain isolated, but often feel better because they have mastered difficult tasks such as course preparations. The entry period (Braskamp, Fowler, & Ory, 1984) seems completed in the third year, although getting sufficient specific feedback on job performance may still be missing. A mentor offering honest evaluative information can be helpful.

- The fourth year brings stability and intellectual stimulation for only about half the faculty studied. By the end of the fourth year, faculty are settling in and their patterns are becoming fixed, for better or worse.

MENTORING

Mentors are teachers, advisors, sponsors, and guides (Levinson, 1978); they provide friendship and intellectual guidance (Sands, Parson, & Duane, 1991). They maintain confidentiality regarding issues raised by the new faculty member. In departments with high levels of conflict, it is important that their focus remain on the person being mentored, not on convincing a new colleague about the merits of one side or the other. Good mentoring allows new colleagues to grow into their professional role as faculty members; it does not keep faculty members in junior roles (Merriam, 1983).

New Faculty Need to Meet and Be Met

Left to their own devices, new faculty are easily overwhelmed with the responsibilities of the next lecture or journal article to read, and many become reclusive. Mentoring can force them out of their offices to meet others in social situations, or at workshops and presentations. These interactions decrease loneliness, develop new relationships, allow a comparison of experiences, and make them feel part of an enterprise larger than themselves.

Assign a Mentor and Require Mentoring

We recommend that a mentor be assigned and that attending departmental or university mentor meetings, orientations, workshops and programs be required. The best mentors are those who can remember their own early years as faculty, know something about the developmental process a new faculty member moves through, want to work with a junior colleague, are proficient in teaching and scholarship, and are familiar with the people and processes in the college or university. Good mentors know that new faculty may be resistant to the idea of taking time away from lecture preparation or scholarship just to talk and are patient; they recognize it will take time to establish a relationship.

Mentoring seems to work best in a one-to-one relationship. It need not be done by senior faculty, nor by someone within the same department. There is value in a mentor from outside the home department, someone not involved in personnel decisions for the new hire, nor with departmental politics.

However, someone within the department needs to work with a new colleague to educate him or her about the history of the department, its current faculty, and its processes and procedures. Even if your university has a mentoring program, we recommend that the department assign a mentor to your new hire. This mentor will need information about the university-level program to complement the information the new hire receives.

Mentoring is Ongoing

It is critical that new faculty members have mentors throughout their probationary period. As they learn their way around and meet their colleagues, new faculty may want to select a different mentor whose work they respect or with whom they have become friends. This is to be encouraged. We recommend that a department mentor, even a temporary one, contact the new hire the day the candidate accepts the offer and answer questions via e-mail or telephone thereafter. A departmental mentor can be invaluable prior to arrival on campus.

Advice for On-Campus Mentors

We recommend the following for on-campus mentors:

- Be prepared. Do some reading on new faculty, good teaching, and successful scholarship. (The recommended readings in this book provide a start.)

- Meet regularly, about every two weeks.

- Provide an orientation for your new colleagues early in their first year. Include a larger perspective (e.g., history of the department or institution) and small details (when book orders are due, what paperwork requests from the chair can be expected during a semester). If the department has more than one new hire, consider a group orientation.

- Meet on or off campus, but within walking distance if possible. Get the new colleague out of the office.

- Do not set an agenda for these meetings. Let the new faculty bring up issues, but be sensitive to what is not being discussed (e.g., struggles with lectures or anxieties about scholarship).

- Exchange honest advice, praise, and criticism.

- Discuss the stress of teaching and the crises which will inevitably occur.

- Know the department and university standards for renewal and tenure so you can ensure that your new colleague is doing the things that need to be done (e.g., use of teaching evaluations, senior faculty visitations to the classroom, beginning service responsibilities).

- Be focused. Your underlying concern must always be with professional development.

Mentoring Responsibilities

Teaching. The mentor should ensure that the new hire receives as much teaching information and material as possible in order to ease the process of beginning several new classes at once in a new teaching environment. The following are things the mentor can do to increase the chances of a successful first year in the classroom, laboratory, or studio.

- Provide a list of relevant films and videotapes, including information on reservations, rental, and purchase.

- Indicate who prepares examinations (e.g., secretary, faculty).

- Provide a book or two on teaching, such as McKeachie' (1994) *Teaching Tips.*

- As the semester unfolds, help the new colleague plan ahead. Having three sets of student papers due from different classes on the same day is not good planning.

- Provide information on the departmental curricula, philosophy, grading practices, and assessment of student outcomes.

- Support risk taking in the classroom. Even if you believe in the lecture format, encourage new faculty to walk into a class prepared to lead a discussion or engage students in an active learning exercise. New teachers need to learn that there are different ways of teaching, and that the world does not end if a lecture is not perfect.

- Assist in coping with student problems such as difficult students in the classroom, complaints about grades, or requests for extra credit.

- Help to interpret and use teaching evaluations to improve teaching.

- Provide opportunities to learn more about teaching at on or off campus forums, conferences, or institutes.

- Assist in developing or revising a teaching portfolio after the first year.

Scholarship or Artistic Performance

Because of the necessity of meeting assigned classes, teaching commands the attention of new faculty. If scholarship or artistic performance suffers in the process, anxiety and concern will begin to rise. We suggest the following:

- Prepare a scholarly activity plan (Freudenthal & DiGiorgio, 1989) to focus attention on the need to be active and manage time effectively.

- Introduce the idea of working on scholarship regularly, even if only a few hours a week. If new faculty feel that scholarship must be done as it was in graduate school, with huge amounts of time and all at once, they will become frustrated and not be productive.

- Have new hires log how their time is actually spent. Discuss it and help them make changes if needed.

- Be honest and supportive regarding standards for renewal and tenure.

- Make sure new faculty receive promised studio or laboratory space and equipment. Oftentimes new faculty are hesitant and/or do not know proper protocol for complaining to a department chair or dean. But as a mentor you do, and you can intervene as appropriate.

- Reduce the isolation of your new colleagues. Read draft manuscripts, review methodological issues prior to data collection, suggest collaborative work, even if on a small scale. And if the new colleague feels shaky about independent scholarship, find a senior research mentor.

- If on-campus funding to support scholarship or artistic performance is available, help your new colleagues apply. Read draft proposals and work with them to increase the chance of success. If they are denied support, help them read feedback honestly and resubmit as soon as possible. Successful scholars all suffer setbacks, but they persevere.

- Suggest conferences where work in progress or supervised undergraduate or graduate scholarship can be presented. Attending gets the new hire off campus, increases networking, and motivates scholarship.

- Provide information on travel policies and support.

- When a new faculty is successful (e.g., artistic performance or journal article), make sure your colleagues know it.

Service, Citizenship, and Personnel Decisions

Some of a mentor's most useful advice involves issues of service, citizenship, and personnel decisions. Some areas of mentoring include:

- Get new hires talking with others. Urge them to schedule one or more hours of collegial talk a week in the faculty lounge or colleagues' offices.

- Discuss how the new hire is getting along with others. Describe department colleagues' styles and quirks.

- Point out alternative ways of handling situations in meetings and committees and how to disagree diplomatically.

- Assist new faculty members in controlling service so they are not overwhelmed by such assignments. Service is usually less important than teaching or scholarship (artistic work) for their first few years.

- Prepare new hires for their first contract renewals. Make them aware of deadlines. Provide a sample of a completed document. Suggest they begin a file for contract reviews and salary decisions, and help organize it.

The Community

Do not underestimate the importance of the non-work environment in determining whether someone decides to stay with you or leave. Some suggestions are:

- Inquire about housing preferences, family, hobbies, etc.

- Make sure new faculty attend department, college, and university social events so they can meet people in a relaxed social atmosphere.

- Inform your new colleagues of campus and community artistic performances, sporting events, and other activities. If you attend, ask them to join you.

Off-Campus Mentoring

Relationships with mentors on other campuses should be encouraged. New faculty need someone to talk with about their career and job, and to provide a perspective on their complaints and achievements.

POINTS OF ENTRY MADE EASY

We recommend providing new faculty members with lists of helpful individuals in various capacities, both on and off campus. Include their titles, phone numbers, and who has a relationship with them (you, another colleague, a spouse). Then when assistance is needed, the new hire has a help list to consult. Make sure these people really do come through for you or others and know what they are doing. Add your own entries to these lists depending on your campus and community. Table 14.1 presents examples of such entry points.

TABLE 14.1

A HELP LIST: INFORMATION FOR NEW FACULTY

On-Campus

- Budget/Accounting (travel forms, reimbursement, etc.)
- Purchasing (advise on competitive bids, getting ordered materials in a timely fashion)
- Computers (purchasing, service, e-mail, networking, etc.)
- Bookstore (ordering books, trouble shooting)
- Media Services (making high quality posters or overheads)
- Library (interlibrary loans, reserving materials)
- Audiovisual (films/tapes for class)
- Document Services (printing exams, manuscripts, etc.)
- Parking (guest speakers, questions on parking tickets)
- Dean of Students (troubled student, cheating, etc.)
- College and/or Graduate Dean's Office (questions on process and procedure)
- Registration (advising students)
- Teaching Excellence Center
- Faculty Development Program
- Personnel (health coverage, W-2 forms, paychecks)
- Campus Credit Union
- The most helpful custodian

Off-Campus

- Physicians, attorneys, dentists, accountant, insurance, etc.
- Restaurants, entertainment, the best pizza in town
- Travel agent

- Real estate agent
- Day care, schools, baby sitters
- Children's activities (academic, sports, etc.)
- Information related to hobbies
- Auto mechanic
- Home repair (plumber, electrician, remodeler, builder, etc.)
- Banking

CHECKLIST

_____ The milieu in which a new faculty works is assessed.

_____ Mentoring process is agreed on.

_____ Needed supports are identified.

_____ A mentor from within the department is assigned.

_____ Development of new faculty is understood.

_____ The new hire is informed about the departmental expectations for participating in mentoring (e.g., it is required, it will be ongoing for several years).

_____ A non-departmental mentor is assigned, if required.

_____ Lists of key points of entry are provided.

_____ New faculty stays, is productive, and obtains tenure.

EXERCISE

The scenario

Dr. N., the assistant professor you hired last year, is sinking fast. Overwhelmed with teaching responsibilities and a summer which involved far more course development and less attention to scholarship than he had planned for, he begins his third semester with little energy and feelings of isolation. He is beginning to talk about no one understanding how hard junior faculty work and the unreasonable pressures they are under.

*Dr. N. is well liked by department members and was hired with
great optimism, but the first year and beginning of his third semester do
not bode well. He has begun little scholarship, his student evaluations
are average at best, and he is beginning to "blame the victim," stating
that his teacher ratings would be higher if students were smarter and
worked harder.*

*Dr. N. has had a rough first year, but no rougher than is experi-
enced by many new hires. He has met with his mentor regularly, and
has honestly disclosed his difficulties. But the feeling is that he is drown-
ing, overwhelmed by what needs to be done, and clearly not performing
well nor enjoying his work.*

- *As a mentor, how would you proceed?*

- *As a member of the department, what would you recommend be
  done to help this new faculty reach his potential and succeed as
  an academician?*

Some answers

Dr. N.'s mentor began by rereading his application materials. His
background and performance had been strong in both teaching and
scholarship. His campus interview was excellent, with a well-prepared
colloquium, an excellently taught class, and positive feedback from students. The mentor then reviewed Boice's (1992) work on the new faculty
member and reflected on what Dr. N. was experiencing. He seemed to be
struggling more than typical new faculty, with little attention to work
beyond his teaching.

The mentor then reviewed brief notes he had kept from his meetings
with Dr. N and a log on how Dr. N spent his time. Guidance had been
offered and suggestions made, but Dr. N. seemed paralyzed, his activities
were not balanced, and his isolation was increasing. The mentor decided a
change was needed; there was little point in continuing the strategies which
were not working.

The mentor began his next meeting with Dr. N. by expressing his concerns and reviewing the first year. He agreed with Dr. N. that he was struggling, but did not agree that teaching would get better if he either worked
harder or if students were different. Using a technique called paradoxical
intervention, he suggested that Dr. N. put everything else aside and write a
perfect lecture for one class for next week. Dr. N. was surprised that his
mentor would give up the mantra of balance, but readily agreed.

At the next meeting Dr. N. was more confused than ever. He had spent six hours polishing and organizing a single 50-minute lecture and the class had gone well, but not unusually so. When asked, Dr. N. admitted that he had received no applause, and students were still fidgeting with their books, ready to leave the class when time expired. Dr. N. realized that this perfect lecture was not substantially better than his other lectures. He was exhausted, convinced that more work was not the answer, and ready to try something different.

Dr. N.'s mentor suggested that he limit lecture and class preparation to an agreed number of hours per week. If he felt that class time would be empty, he was to quickly write some questions for discussion, invite someone in for a mini-guest lecture, review what had been discussed, answer questions, or just "wing it." The mentor said that he would be disappointed if Dr. N. stayed with an all-lecture format in his courses. Also, his mentor suggested that he schedule two hours of free time a week, to be filled by wandering and visiting. The more time he spent in other people's offices, labs, or studios the better.

As the semester progressed, Dr. N. began to loosen up. When he discovered that the perfect lecture was mythical, he could move on and set aside small amounts of regular time for scholarship. In addition, his anger began to dissipate, and he felt less trapped by his teaching. Interestingly, his students responded more positively to his more relaxed teaching style and the small amounts of variety he had introduced into his classes. The department faculty began to believe they could avoid another recruitment.

REFERENCES AND RECOMMENDED READINGS

Boice, R. (1992). *The new faculty member: Supporting and fostering professional development.* San Francisco, CA: Jossey-Bass.

Braskamp, L. A., Fowler, D. L., & Ory, J. C. (1984). Faculty development and achievement: A faculty's view. *Review of Higher Education, 7,* 205-222.

Davidson, C.I., & Ambrose, S. A. (1994). *The new professor's handbook: A guide to teaching and research in engineering and science.* Bolton, MA: Anker.

Diamond, R. M. (1994). *Serving on promotion and tenure committees: A faculty guide.* Bolton, MA: Anker.

Diamond, R. M. (1995). *Preparing for promotion and tenure review: A faculty guide.* Bolton, MA: Anker.

Elson, J. A. (1989). Mandatory teaching effectiveness workshops for new faculty: What a difference three years make. *Journal of Staff, Program, and Organization Development, 7*, 59-66.

Fink, L. D. (1990). New faculty members: The professoriate of tomorrow. *Journal of Staff, Program, and Organization Development, 8*, 235-245.

Freudenthal, N. R., & DiGiorgio, A. J. (1989). New faculty mentoring: The institution as mentor. *Journal of Staff, Program, and Organization Development, 7*, 67-71.

Gibson, G. W. (1992). *Good start: A guidebook for new faculty in liberal arts colleges.* Bolton, MA: Anker.

Hofsess, D. (1990). The power of mentoring: A moving force in staff development. *Journal of Staff Development, 11*(2), 20-24.

Lavery, P. T., Boice, R., Thompson, R. W., & Turner, J. L. (1989). Mentoring for new faculty. *Journal of Staff, Program, and Organization Development, 7*, 39-46.

Levinson, D. J. (1978). *The seasons of a man's life.* New York, NY: Knopf.

Lewis, K. G., Svinicki, M. D., & Stice, J. E. (1985). Filling the gap: Introducing new faculty to the basics of teaching. *Journal of Staff, Program, and Organization Development, 3*, 16-21.

McKeachie, W. J. (1994). *Teaching tips: Strategies, research, and theory for college and university teachers (9th ed.).* Lexington, MA: D. C. Heath.

Merriam, S. (1983). Mentors and protégés: A critical review of the literature. *Adult Education Quarterly, 33*, 161-173.

Sands, R. G., Parson, L. A., & Duanne, J. (1991). Faculty mentoring faculty in a public university. *Journal of Higher Education, 62*, 174-193.

Schuster, J. H., Wheeler, D. W., et al. (Eds.). (1990). *Enhancing faculty careers: Strategies for development and renewal.* San Francisco, CA: Jossey-Bass.

Seldin, P., & Associates. (1995). *Improving college teaching.* Bolton, MA: Anker.

Wood, F. H., & Thompson, S. R. (1993). Assumptions about staff development based on research and best practice. *Journal of Staff Development, 14*(4), 52-57.

Wright, W. A. & Associates. (1995). *Teaching improvement practices: Successful strategies for higher education.* Bolton, MA: Anker.

BIBLIOGRAPHY

American Association of University Professors. (1990). *Policy documents and reports*. Washington, DC: Author.

Arreola, R. A. (1995). *Developing a comprehensive faculty evaluation system: A handbook for college faculty and administrators on designing and operating a comprehensive faculty evaluation system*. Bolton, MA: Anker.

Barzun, J. (1991). *Begin here*. Chicago, IL: The University of Chicago Press.

Bloom, A. (1987). *The closing of the American mind*. New York, NY: Touchstone.

Boice, R. (1991). New faculty as teachers. *Journal of Higher Education, 62*, 150-173.

Boice, R. (1992). *The new faculty member: Supporting and fostering professional development*. San Francisco, CA: Jossey-Bass.

Bowen, H. R. (1982). *The state of the nation and the agenda for higher education*. San Francisco, CA: Jossey-Bass.

Bowen, H. R., & Schuster, J. H. (1986). *American professors: A national resource imperiled*. New York, NY: Oxford University Press.

Boyer, E. L. (1987). *The undergraduate experience in America*. New York, NY: Harper & Row.

Boyer, E. L. (1990). *Scholarship reconsidered: Priorities of the professoriate*. Princeton, NJ: Carnegie Foundation for the Advancement of Teaching.

Braskamp, L. A., Fowler, D. L., & Ory, J. C. (1984). Faculty development and achievement: A faculty's view. *Review of Higher Education, 7*, 205-222.

Brookfield, S. D. (1990). *The skillful teacher: On technique, trust, and responsiveness in the classroom*. San Francisco, CA: Jossey-Bass.

Burke, D. L. (1987). The academic marketplace in the 1980s: Appointment and termination of assistant professors. *The Review of Higher Education, 10*, 199-214.

Caplow, T., & McGee, R. J. (1958). *The academic marketplace.* New York, NY: Basic Books.

Carnegie Foundation for the Advancement of Teaching. (1981). *Three thousand futures: The next twenty-five years for higher education.* San Francisco, CA: Jossey-Bass.

Centra, J. A. (1994). The use of the teaching portfolio and student evaluations for summative evaluation. *Journal of Higher Education, 65,* 555-570.

Chicago Tribune. (1992, June 21-25). *Degrees of Neglect: Our Failing Colleges.*

Clark, B. R., (1987). *The academic life: Small worlds, different worlds.* Princeton, NJ: Carnegie Foundation for the Advancement of Teaching.

Clark, S. M., & Lewis, D. R. (Eds.). (1985). *Faculty vitality and institutional productivity: Critical perspectives for higher education.* New York, NY: Teachers College Press.

Cornwall, J. R., & Perlman, B. (1990). *Organizational entrepreneurship.* Homewood, IL: Irwin.

Council of Colleges of Arts and Sciences. (1992). *The ethics of recruitment and faculty appointment.* Columbus, OH: The Ohio State University.

Davidson, C.I., & Ambrose, S. A. (1994). *The new professor's handbook: A guide to teaching and research in engineering and science.* Bolton, MA: Anker.

Davis, B. G. (1993). *Tools for teaching.* San Francisco, CA: Jossey-Bass.

Deal, T. E., & Kennedy, A. A. (1982). *Corporate cultures.* Reading, MA: Addison-Wesley.

Deneef, A. L, Goodwin, C. D., & McCrate, E. S. (Eds.). (1988). *The academic's handbook.* Durham, NC: Duke University Press.

Diamond, R. M. (1994). *Serving on promotion and tenure committees: A faculty guide.* Bolton, MA: Anker.

Diamond, R. M. (1995). *Preparing for promotion and tenure review: A faculty guide.* Bolton, MA: Anker.

Diamond, R. M., & Gray, P. (1987, January). *National study of teaching assistants (Tech. Rep.).* Syracuse, NY: Syracuse University Center for Instructional Development.

Dill, D. D. (Ed.). Ethics and the academic profession. *Journal of Higher Education, 53,* 243-381.

Duffy, D. K., & Jones, J. W. (1995). *Teaching within the rhythms of the semester.* San Francisco, CA: Jossey-Bass.

Eble, K. E. (1976). *The craft of teaching.* San Francisco, CA: Jossey-Bass.

Eble, K. E., & McKeachie, W. J. (1985). *Improving undergraduate education through faculty development.* San Francisco, CA: Jossey-Bass.

Edgerton, R., Hutchings, P., & Quinlan, K. (1991). *The teaching portfolio: Capturing the scholarship in teaching.* Washington, DC: American Association for Higher Education.

Elson, J. A. (1989). Mandatory teaching effectiveness workshops for new faculty: What a difference three years make. *Journal of Staff, Program, and Organization Development, 7,* 59-66.

Ericksen, S. (1984). *The essence of good teaching.* San Francisco, CA: Jossey-Bass.

Erickson, B. L., & Strommer, D. W. (1991). *Teaching college freshmen.* San Francisco, CA: Jossey-Bass.

Fink, L. D. (1984). *The first year of college teaching.* San Francisco, CA: Jossey-Bass.

Fink, L. D. (1990). New faculty members: The professoriate of tomorrow. *Journal of Staff, Program, and Organization Development, 8,* 235-245.

Flood, B. J., & Moll, J. K. (1990). *The professor business: A teaching primer for faculty.* Medford, NJ: Learned Information.

Freudenthal, N. R., & DiGiorgio, A. J. (1989). New faculty mentoring: The institution as mentor. *Journal of Staff, Program, and Organization Development, 7,* 67-71.

Gaff, J. G. (1975). *Toward faculty renewal.* San Francisco, CA: Jossey-Bass.

Getman, J. (1992). *In the company of scholars: The struggle for the soul of higher education.* Austin, TX: University of Texas Press.

Gibson, G. W. (1992). *Good start: A guidebook for new faculty in liberal arts colleges.* Bolton, MA: Anker.

Gullette, M. M. (Ed.). (1984). *The art and craft of teaching.* Cambridge, MA: Harvard University Press.

Hofsess, D. (1990). The power of mentoring: A moving force in staff development. *Journal of Staff Development, 11*(2), 20-24.

Keith-Spiegel, P., Wittig, A. R., Perkins, D. V., Balogh, D. W., & Whitley Jr., B. E. (1993). *The ethics of teaching: A casebook.* Muncie, IN: Ball State University.

Kuhn, R. L. (Ed.). (1988). *Handbook for creative and innovative managers.* New York, NY: McGraw-Hill.

Lambert, L., & Tice, S. (Eds.) (1993). *Preparing graduate students to teach.* Washington, DC: American Association for Higher Education.

Lavery, P. T., Boice, R., Thompson, R. W., & Turner, J. L. (1989). Mentoring for new faculty. *Journal of Staff, Program, and Organization Development, 7,* 39-46.

Levinson, D. J. (1978). *The seasons of a man's life.* New York, NY: Knopf.

Lewis, K. G., Svinicki, M. D., & Stice, J. E. (1985). Filling the gap: Introducing new faculty to the basics of teaching. *Journal of Staff, Program, and Organization Development, 3,* 16-21.

Lowman, J. (1984). *Mastering the techniques of teaching.* San Francisco, CA: Jossey-Bass.

Marchese, T. J., & Lawrence, J. F. (1988). *The search committee handbook: A guide to recruiting administrators.* Washington, DC: American Association for Higher Education.

Markie, P. J. (1994). *Professor's duties: Ethical issues in college teaching.* Lanham, MD: Rowman & Littlefield.

May, W. W. (Ed.). (1990). *Ethics and higher education.* New York, NY: Macmillan.

McFadden, S., & Perlman, B. (1989). Faculty recruitment and excellent undergraduate teaching. *Teaching of Psychology, 16,* 195-198.

McKeachie, W. J. (1994). *Teaching tips: Strategies, research, and theory for college and university teachers (9th ed.).* Lexington, MA: D.C. Heath.

Merriam, S. (1983). Mentors and protégés: A critical review of the literature. *Adult Education Quarterly, 33,* 161-173.

Mueller, A., Perlman, B., McCann, L. I., & McFadden, S. (1996, January). *Teaching assistant training in psychology—1994 study.* Poster presented at the 18th Annual Institute for the Teaching of Psychology, St. Petersburg Beach, FL.

New Directions for Teaching and Learning. Quarterly journal. San Francisco, CA: Jossey-Bass.

Newble, D., & Cannon, R. (1989). *A handbook for teachers in universities and colleges: A guide to improving teaching methods.* New York, NY: St. Martin's Press.

Nyquist, J. D., Abbott, R. D., Wulff, D. H., & Sprague, J. (Eds.). (1991). *Preparing the professoriate of tomorrow to teach: Selected readings in TA training.* Dubuque, IA: Kendall/Hunt.

Perlman, B., & McCann, L. I. (1993). The place of mathematics and science in undergraduate psychology education. *Teaching of Psychology, 20,* 205-209.

Perlman, B., Gueths, J., & Weber, D. A. (1988). *The academic intrapreneur: Strategy, innovation, and management in higher education.* New York, NY: Praeger.

Perlman, B., Konop, K., McFadden, S., & McCann, L. I. (1996, January). *A study of the faculty teaching role.* Poster presented at the 18th Annual Institute for the Teaching of Psychology, St. Petersburg Beach, FL.

Perlman, B., Marxen, J. C., McFadden, S., & McCann, L. I. (in press). Applicants for a faculty position do not emphasize teaching, *Teaching of Psychology.*

Professional and Organizational Development Network in Higher Education. (1984). *To improve the academy: Volume III.* Pittsburgh, PA: POD.

Ray, M., & Myers, R. (1986). *Creativity in business.* Garden City, NY: Doubleday.

Ross, R. D. (1981, May). The fine art of faculty recruitment. *Music Educators Journal, 67,* 49-51.

Sands, R. G., Parson, L. A., & Duanne, J. (1991). Faculty mentoring faculty in a public university. *Journal of Higher Education, 62,* 174-193.

Schein, E. H. (1985). *Organizational culture and leadership.* San Francisco, CA: Jossey-Bass.

Schuster, J. H., Wheeler, D. W., et al. (Eds.). (1990). *Enhancing faculty careers: Strategies for development and renewal.* San Francisco, CA: Jossey-Bass.

Seldin, P. (1991). *The teaching portfolio: A practical guide to improved performance and promotion/tenure decisions.* Bolton, MA: Anker.

Seldin, P., & Associates. (1993). *Successful use of teaching portfolios.* Bolton, MA: Anker.

Seldin, P., & Associates. (1995). *Improving college teaching.* Bolton, MA: Anker.

Shore, M. B., and others. (1986). *The teaching dossier (rev. ed.).* Montreal, Quebec: Canadian Association of University Teachers.

Smith, P. (1990). *Killing the spirit: Higher education in America.* New York, NY: Viking.

Sommerfeld, R., & Nagely, D. (1974). Seek and ye shall find: The organization and conduct of a search committee. *Journal of Higher Education, 45,* 239-252.

Steininger, M., Newell, J. D., & Garcia, L. T. (1984). *Ethical issues in psychology.* Homewood, IL: Dorsey Press.

Stoner, C. R., & Fry, F. L. (1987). *Strategic planning in the small business.* Cincinnati, OH: South-Western.

Sykes, C. J. (1986). *Profscam.* New York, NY: St. Martin's Press.

Taylor, B. R. (1991). *Affirmative action at work: Law, politics, and ethics.* Pittsburgh, PA: University of Pittsburgh Press.

Thompson, F., & Zumeta, W. (1985). Hiring decisions in organized anarchies: More evidence on entrance into the academic career. *The Review of Higher Education, 8,* 123-138.

Trela, D. J. (1989, March 29). Academic indignities. *Chronicle of Higher Education,* pp. B3-B4.

Van Note Chism, N. (Ed.). (1987). *Institutional responsibilities and responses in the employment and education of teaching assistants: Readings from a national conference.* Columbus, OH: The Ohio State University Center for Teaching Excellence.

Waggaman, J. S. (1983). *Faculty recruitment, retention and fair employment: Obligations and opportunities.* ASHE-ERIC Higher Education Research Report No. 2, Washington, DC: Association for the Study of Higher Education.

Warch, R. (1992). *Practicing what we preach: Scholarship and the aims of a liberal arts education.* 1991-1992 President's Report. Appleton, WI: Lawrence University, pp. 3-9.

Weimer, M. (1988). Reading your way to better teaching. *College Teaching, 36*(2), 48-53.

Weimer, M. (1990). *Improving college teaching: Strategies for developing instructional effectiveness.* San Francisco, CA: Jossey-Bass.

Winston, G. C. (1994, September/October). Teaching: Moral failure or market pressure? *Change,* 9-15.

Wood, F. H., & Thompson, S. R. (1993). Assumptions about staff development based on research and best practice. *Journal of Staff Development, 14*(4), 52-57.

Wright, W. A., & Associates. (1995). *Teaching improvement practices: Successful strategies for higher education.* Bolton, MA: Anker.

Zanna, M. P., & Darley, J. M. (Eds.). (1987). *The compleat academic: A practical guide for the beginning social scientist.* Hillsdale, NJ: Lawrence Erlbaum.

INDEX

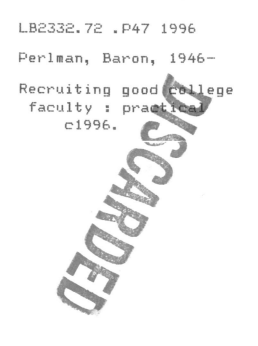